newly revise  **d**

S0-BKA-018

internet
for
christians

Quentin J. Schultze

everything you need
to start cruising the
net today

GOSPEL FILMS
PUBLICATIONS

© Copyright 1996, Gospel Films, Inc. Box 455; Muskegon, MI 49443-0455 616-773-3361
Toll Free: 1-800-253-0413 fax: 616-777-1847 Internet URL: http://www.gospelcom.net

DEDICATED

TO THREE

CHRISTIAN VISIONARIES:

—

ED PRINCE
THE LATE BUSINESSMAN, PHILANTHROPIST, AND
GOSPEL FILMS BOARD SECRETARY

RICH DEVOS
CO-FOUNDER OF AMWAY AND
GOSPEL FILMS BOARD CHAIRMAN

BILLY ZEOLI
GOSPEL FILMS PRESIDENT

Acknowledgements

I'm grateful for all of the people who helped make this book possible.

My family is filled with love and talent. My wife, Barbara, deserves much applause for her unswerving support, encouragement and editorial skill. She could have been a writer or editor. Son Steve did much of the computer work for the appendix. His energy and computer prowess are incredible. He stands above me in more than height.

My students at Calvin College are a constant source of excitement and helpful questions. The interns of the summer of 1995 were guinea pigs for much of the material in this book. I thank them all — David Korff, Andy Padjen, Brian Poel, Russ Roozeboom, Scott Stegenga, and especially Rodney Van Zee, who read the entire manuscript as an Internet user, "PK," and budding web-site designer. Scott deserves special credit for his excellent work on the online version of the appendix.

Charlie Peacock and Nick Barre's enthusiasm for the new media helped give me hope for both Christian and artistic uses of digital communication. Their colleague in recording and NetCentral president, Craig Hansen, gave similar hope. I pray that this book will do some justice to their vision.

My colleague at Calvin, Robert Fortner, always the smiling skeptic, provided an ongoing prophetic edge to my thoughts and reflections. He is more than a friend.

I am continually helped by the superb preaching of my pastor, Jack Roeda, who can know little of the lasting impact of his ministry on the people he serves with humility and truth. He needs no computer to preach like a giant.

Smitty at Gospel Films believed in this project from the beginning, even though he was never sure of the outcome. His trust is greatly appreciated. So is his attention to frustrating details and his willingness to consider the perpetual pontificating provided by my professional pronouncements.

The Gospel Communications Network deserves the accolades I offer in this book. The crew there is remarkably creative and adventurous. They tried many of my unproven ideas. May God Bless their courage, even if my ideas were sometimes half-baked.

Warren Kramer, graphic designer extraordinaire, created the look and feel of this book. Thanks, from "Dr. Q."

The dedication speaks for itself. To God be the glory, on earth and in heaven. It's all Grace.

T A B L E   O F
Contents

1: "What is 'surfing the Net?'"

2: "I'm scared to death of computers. Whenever I use one, I get sweaty palms and heart palpitations. What will happen to me if I get on the Internet?"

3: "I keep hearing and reading about all kinds of technical stuff that doesn't make any sense to me — FTP, telnet, domain name and so on. Do I have to master this kind of technical jargon to use the Internet?"

4: "I've heard that the Internet is nothing but a bunch of undecipherable research reports. Why should I go through all of the hassles of getting on the Net only to read government-funded studies about the mating habits of Ethiopian fruit flies?"

5: "We're a young couple with small children. We care about family values. Should we really let our kids get on the Internet?"

6: "Isn't the Internet just a fad — like the video game we bought that now sits unused in the basement?"

7: "Do we really need computers and the Internet? Isn't all of this computer stuff poor stewardship of our limited time and money?"

8: "I've read all kinds of stories in the paper about people breaking into Internet computers and stealing private information like credit-card numbers. If my family gets on the Internet, can people get information about us?"

9: "Given all of the publicity about smut dealers on the computer networks, and even attempted child luring, is it safe for any children to be on?"

10: "One of my friends tried for months to get hooked up to the Internet. He finally gave up in frustration. Is it really so hard to get on?"

11: "I heard that e-mail addresses could be the Mark of the Beast. What do you think?"

12: "I own a Christian business and considered selling my products on the Internet until someone told me that commerce is discouraged. Is that true?"

13: "I work for a large missions organization involved in international outreach. Is the Internet a reliable way for us to communicate with missionaries and nationals around the world?"

14: "Our pastor says that he was not taught anything about computers and the Internet in seminary. He also says that he can't imagine that computers could really help him pastor our church. Why should we help him get on the Internet?"

15: "I read recently that a group in Europe is predicting that the Internet will soon stop working because of all of the people using it. Why should Christians get involved in a medium that may come crashing down, anyway?"

Two: Welcome to the "Inter-what?"

Is There Really an Internet?

What's the Infosuperhighway?

So What Is the Internet, Anyway?

Mailing Lists

What Are Mailing Lists? How Do I Subscribe?

Lists for All Christians

Lists for Ministry Leaders, including Parish Pastors, Student Leaders, Youth Leaders, Chaplains and Missionaries

Lists for Christian Scholars and Other Academic-Minded Folks, including Theologians

Lists for Christian Traditions

Where Can I Find More Mailing Lists?

P R E F A C E

Looking for Internet Saints

The word "Internet" is so widely used and misused these days that many people just shrug their shoulders in confusion whenever they hear or read it. I recently used the term in a public presentation, only to have someone respond, "The inter-what?" Good question!

After another presentation someone asked me if Christians should be associated with the Internet, given all of the bad publicity about the Internet's smut dealers, invasions of privacy, information about how to make bombs like the one used to blow up the federal building in Oklahoma City, attempted luring of children via the Internet, and so on.

Oddly enough, just a few weeks earlier I had spoken at a major seminary where many students took class notes from laptop computers. After class quite a few of these current and future pastors told me about how they used the Internet for theological research, pastoral discussions with other clergy, e-mail with parishioners and distant family, and much more. These are the two faces of the "Net" — one repulsive and one attractive, one that reflects goodness and Grace, and the other that displays human sinfulness.

Years ago Christians looked suspiciously at Hollywood. There were plenty of reasons to let others rule the movie roost, from the morally bankrupt films to the lifestyles of some of the more notorious movie stars. In hindsight, however, the decision to forsake Hollywood merely led to a forsaken Hollywood. *There comes a time when the church of Jesus Christ has to be bold enough to lay claim to a new medium.* As I like to put it, new technologies are part of the unfolding of God's Creation. We don't own these technologies; God does. We're stewards,

caretakers and representatives on behalf of the King of Kings. You and I
have inherited God's command to Adam to take care of and develop the
Creation.

Of course this is no easy commandment to fully obey. Our shal-
low declarations about the sovereignty of God over the entire Creation
can turn into triumphalistic babble about how great Christians are to be
using new technologies. This was the problem in Babel, wasn't it? They
were the technocrats of their age. They were going to communicate directly with God by building the tower into the heavens — a tower built
of man-made stuff and with man-made pride. Let's not let our own
pride, our dreams of personal power and glory, get in the way of our
work toward redeeming the media, including the Internet.

> **"The Internet is a worldwide network of computer net-
> works. It enables people to communicate via computer
> using text, sound and images ."**

The Net is no longer a medium just for computer specialists or
technically inclined people. It's being used by people in government, education, business, ministry, and practically all other areas of work. It's
also becoming an entertainment medium, providing hours of fun to millions of people. In addition, the Internet is rapidly being transformed
into what may become the major news and information medium of the
late 20th and early 21st centuries. Thousands of libraries, research centers, health-information institutes and periodicals are now on the
Internet (or "online," as some people say).

The big turning point in the life of the Internet is the World Wide
Web (WWW or simply the "Web"). The Web is an easy, intuitive, visual
way of using the Internet that anyone can learn in a few minutes. The Web
does not now include everything on the Internet, but it is rapidly becoming the "vehicle" of choice for people who use the Net. The Web lets you
travel or "surf" the Net with ease, communicating with people and organizations all over the world. You don't have to know all kinds of "addresses"
or technical jargon to use the Web.

There is no doubt that the Web will entice tens of millions of
people to the Internet. Estimates suggest that the number of people on
the Web is growing by hundreds of thousands every month! If the op-

portunity to use e-mail (electronic mail sent from computer to computer) lures many people to the Internet, the Web gets them hooked. The Web is simply a lot of fun as well as a tremendous resource for information. This book emphasizes e-mail and the Web, the two ways of using the Internet that will undoubtedly be of greatest value to Christians.

There are leading Christian ministries on the Internet. At the Gospel Communications Network (GCN) site, for example, there is an array of Internet resources to minister to people and to help people minister to others. GCN (Web address: http://www.gospelcom.net) is an alliance of far-sighted ministries, including Gospel Films, RBC Ministries (e.g., *Our Daily Bread* and *Sports Spectrum*), Renewing Your Mind with R.C. Sproul, InterVarsity Christian Fellowship (including InterVarsity Press), Children's Bible Hour (*Keys for Kids* radio and devotional), Youth for Christ, Youth Specialties, Navigators (including NavPress), Words of Hope and the long-standing International Bible Society.

GCN provides on the Internet everything from daily devotionals (*Words of Hope, Our Daily Bread, Keys for Kids,* Gospel Films' evangelistic devotional *Daily Wisdom,* etc.) to sample book chapters, ministry resource catalogs, discussion or "mailing lists" for people to join, information about how to defend your faith and to witness to unbelievers, television and radio program schedules, a Christian cartoon (Gospel Films' *Reverend Fun*), articles about Christians in sports (*Sports Spectrum*), convention schedules and calendars, directories to Internet resources for youth ministries, and even a regular news column on what's new on the Internet for Christians — my own *Internet for Christians* site (http://www.gospelcom.net/ifc/). Surely these kinds of activities are a small step toward providing a Godly presence on the Net.

I could add all kinds of Christian sites to this list, but the appendix includes the Net addresses to online directories that will give you many hours of pleasure and edification.

"This book is written for two reasons: First, to get you on the Internet. Second, to make you wise enough to be salt and light in the new medium."

For those of you who simply can't wait to get online, go ahead and turn to chapter four. Use the appendix of this book to find addresses of sites that you would most like to visit. But please read the rest of the book after you finish your first session on the Web. The resources and perspectives discussed in this book will help make your Internet travels much more enjoyable and discerning. More than that, I hope that this book will give you enough knowledge to teach other Christians about the Internet — to get your friends, family, church and other Christian associates online.

If you don't currently have an Internet connection, first read chapter three. Then make some calls (as discussed in that chapter) to locate an Internet access provider in your area. Let that provider give you the necessary software and help you get connected for your first session. Within a day or two you should be able to get on the Web and start sending e-mail.

The Internet is addictive for many people. The Web, in particular, is a tremendous amount of fun. Not surprisingly, people on the Internet have a term to describe people whose whole life seems to revolve around the Net: geeks. These geeks use all of the jargon of the Internet like theologians discuss premillenialism or debate predestination. I suppose the church is served by some Christian Internet geeks.

"I would like to propose that instead of more Internet geeks, the church needs more *Internet saints* — believers who purposely and prayerfully use the new medium selflessly in service of the Kingdom of God."

So I welcome all saints to the world of the Internet. It's a "place" with its own jargon, its own people and its own technology. In spite of what you may think, the Internet is not hard to understand. I'll be your guide, surfing ("travelling," in Internet lingo) through the Net, as its often called. I promise to minimize the jargon and maximize the straight talk about one of the most important technologies of our day.

Then again, if you like the jargon, don't give up on this book. Even if you know the lingo, I'll help you gain a Christian *perspective* on the Internet. Perspective, like wisdom, is a lot harder to find than technical jargon and computer lingo.

Ready? Let's jump into the FAQs.

CHAPTER ONE

Frequently Asked Questions (FAQs) About the Internet

The Internet is loaded with areas dedicated to FAQs (frequently-asked questions) that answer just about every question you could imagine. So here's my own version of FAQs — for Christians who are now on the Net or thinking about getting on it. These questions and answers will give you an introduction to some of the material covered in this book. I also hope that they tickle your funny bone a bit. The Net is serious business, but we often take it too seriously. God is in charge, in spite of our pretentiousness about technology, including computers. Many of these questions have been asked of me in public meetings and private conversations. My apologies to anyone who recognizes their own question in this chapter. I hope that my answers in the book are better than my spontaneous answers over coffee or in public settings.

Question 1: "What is 'surfing the Net?'"

I've got a theory on this. Computers really took off in California, which gave us things like Silicon Valley (which in my view should really be called "Cement Valley" or "High-Tax-No-Parking Ville"). Some long-forgotten Californian used his computer to search the Internet for the best surfing beaches in the world. He called such important research "surfin'." Pretty soon his or her computer-crazed friends began using the same term for all computer-to-computer communication done in a leisurely manner.

Nowadays people use the term "surfing" to refer to the way that people use their computers to search around the Internet for anything unusual or interesting. It's like flipping through channels with the remote control — "channel surfing" the TV. Chapter four gives you lots of tips for finding people, places and resources on the Net, to make your surf less tiring and more fun.

Question 2: "I'm scared to death of computers. Whenever I use one, I get sweaty palms and heart palpitations. What will happen to me if I get on the Internet?"

If you're over 40, heart palpitations and anxiety attacks are natural reactions to computers. God didn't put computers in the Garden of Eden. He put natural, bucolic stuff there, like lions, rattlesnakes and gorillas.

Seriously, computers are no more natural to learn than another language. The older you are, the harder it can be. But don't let fear keep you away from computers or drive you off the Net. Once you learn a few basics, you can surf the Net with the best of them. Remember this: You get to decide how fast or how slowly you surf the Net. And you can't do damage to other peoples' computers when you're surfing to those computers around the world. Chapter one provides a short overview of the so-called infosuperhighway, digital communication and the like. I explain this stuff in a way that should reduce fears.

So relax, and take your time! Enjoy your new computer abilities by visiting the sites that you're most interested in — like where to get inexpensive new bifocals, how to deal with restless-leg syndrome, and how to keep a spouse from complaining about all of your time on the computer.

Question 3: "I keep hearing and reading about all kinds of technical stuff that doesn't make any sense to me — FTP, telnet, domain name and so on. Do I have to master this kind of technical jargon to use the Internet?"

What technical jargon? Just check out the FAQs at the home pages of the NCSA, or FTP to Unix at goobertooter under rotorooter. E-mail answers are available at the following address: <huh@gobbledy-gook.yep>.

No, you don't have to master all of that jargon. I try not to let it get in the way of my use of the Net. The Net has reached the stage when the average person can get hooked up and surfing within minutes, without ever knowing any of the technical phrases. If you'd like to pick up the lingo, then pay attention to such terms, ask questions, and read the FAQs (frequently-asked questions, remember?) at various places on the Net. The Net is no longer just for computer pros or highly technical people.

This book is based on the assumption that to get nearly full use of the Internet as a Christian you'll need only to access e-mail (electronic messages sent from person to person) and the World Wide Web (or just the "Web"). E-mail is very simple to master. The Web is nearly as simple. It uses a visual, graphic means of showing you where you can surf on the Net. All you have to do on the Web is "click" your mouse on the name or picture of the "place" you want to go and — zip!!!— you're automatically connected to the computer located at that place.

If you want to get back to the previous page, you simply click on the "page back" or "back arrow" or equivalent button on the top of your Web-surfing (browser) software. The way the Web works, your computer stores the addresses of the locations you've visited until you turn off (shut down) the browser program. So you could actually go back ten pages with ten clicks of your mouse.

The Web uses what are called hypermedia. It's the same "surfing" technique you'll find on CD-ROM encyclopedias and the like. Some words or phrases are marked with a different color, indicating that if you click the mouse on them you can "go to" that topic. This is hypertext (the underlined words on the back of this book are illustrated exactly as hypertext looks on the Web). Also, particular images, icons or other graphics serve the same function; you click on the graphics and are automatically connected with the computer that gives you information about the image (e.g., a map of a state might give you a place to click to get information about the individual cities or counties). The appendix provides all kinds of Internet addresses for you to "access" directly, without even having to surf around via hypermedia.

Question 4: "I've heard that the Internet is nothing but a bunch of undecipherable research reports. Why should I go through all of the hassles of getting on the Net only to read government-funded studies about the mating habits of

Ethiopian fruit flies?"

I wonder if the fruit flies feel the same way about things. Maybe they need those studies?

Who told you this? It must have been one of those egghead Ph.D.s (read my credits on the back of the book). Once upon a time the Internet was almost exclusively a medium for scholars and researchers. During the last two years this has changed so quickly that there is now far more non-technical, non-academic material on the Net. You'll find the Net loaded with information, ideas, poetry, periodicals, and so forth. You'll discover hundreds of resources for Bible and theological study. You'll run across online malls, movie reviews (and video samples of movies), chatter about the latest news reports, cooking, gardening and seeker churches. The Net is like an enormous flea market of information, entertainment and inspiration.

The appendix gives you an overview of some of the things available on the Net, especially things of interest to Christians. But you really have to get on the Net to believe the scope of it. You might even find those studies about the fruit flies, if you're interested.

Question 5: "We're a young couple with small children. We care about family values. Should we really let our kids get on the Internet?"

You have a valid concern. I'm grateful that you wish to raise your children in the best possible atmosphere, with Godly values and Christian beliefs.

The problem is that the Internet is not going to disappear. The Net is becoming the next major communications medium. Your children will have to learn not only how to navigate the Net, but how to use the Net wisely, with discernment and strong Biblical convictions. How can they do this if they know nothing about the Net?

Another option, if you're comfortable with it, would be to introduce online services slowly to your children. In fact, you can learn the Net along with your kids. Monitor what they do with the computer, keeping the computer located in an open area so that you can easily and frequently check on what's happening. Also, find the best sites for your kids. Believe me, there is wonderful stuff on the Net for Christians and Christian children, including daily devotionals such as Children's Bible Hour's *Keys for Kids.* This way you might be better able to prepare your children for the real world of computers. But don't do it if you're not comfortable with such a plan, or if you simply don't feel able to help the kids make Christian sense out of the Net. Just remember: a time will come when your children will get on the Internet from school, a local library or friends' homes. If you're willing to give it a try, chapter six provides many suggestions for families using the Net from their homes.

Question 6: "Isn't the Internet just a fad — like the video game we bought that now sits unused in the basement?"

If this were true, I wouldn't be writing a book about the Internet and encouraging Christian ministries to get online. The particular technologies now used to surf the Net are probably somewhat faddish. So is the nutty reporting about the Internet that you see and read in the popular media. The Internet is not the "killer medium" that will usher in the "infosuperhighway" and eliminate radio, television, newspapers, books, conversation and hot dogs. Christians should be leery of any reports that paint the Internet like a savior of schools and underprivileged kids. In chapter two, I take on the reporters of this type of very faddish nonsense.

The Internet is the first big wave of a technological revolution. This revolution is nothing more than computer-to-computer communication, also called "digital communication." Computers convert text, sound and images into digital information (don't worry about what "digital" means). It is becoming increasingly inexpensive to send and receive messages of all kinds via computers.

The Internet lets people hook up their computers to other computers, thereby creating a huge, worldwide "network of computer networks" (the "Internet"). This kind of communication is not really a fad, in spite of how faddish the reporting is about the Internet. When you renew your drivers license, charge a purchase with a credit card, "scan" your groceries at the checkout counter of the local supermarket, read the stock-market prices in the paper, and millions of other activities, you are participating directly or indirectly in digital communication. More and more of the communication about products, services, people and events is digital (computer-to-computer communication). The Net is simply one example of this digital revolution taking place all over the world.

Question 7: "Do we really need computers and the Internet? Isn't all of this computer stuff poor stewardship of our limited time and money?"

What do you mean poor stewardship? Just because I mortgaged my house, let my car insurance lapse, and sell ten quarts of each of my children's blood every year to make the computer payments? Come on! No one spends an arm and a leg — or at least not a leg — to get on the Internet!

Stewardship issues are very important considerations when one gets involved in computers. Computer technology can be very expensive and it certainly goes out of date quickly. There's always new software, bigger memories, faster computers and attractive paraphernalia to add on to your computer system.

But the Internet doesn't require top-of-the line computer equipment, as I show in chapter three. Moreover, access to the Internet is increasingly inexpensive. Believe it or not, once you get on the Net you have access to all kinds of free software. Much of the best Internet-related software is *freeware* (entirely free) or *shareware* (pay a small charge for use).

The time issue is trickier to contend with in most families today. Do we now use our time in a stewardly fashion, or do we squander most of our leisure time on fairly selfish pursuits? Will computers and the Net make this situation better or worse? I think that each family has to make some tough choices about these matters.

Question 8: "I've read all kinds of stories in the paper about people breaking into Internet computers and stealing private information like credit-card numbers. If my family gets on the Internet, can people get information about us?"

Once again, the media have jumped on small stories and turned them into big issues. Yes, there are breaches of security on the Net. No, people cannot break into your computer and steal all kinds of private information from your family's computer system.

The Internet is simply a network of computer networks. When you get on the Net, you tap into these networks and retrieve information from *other* computers. Normally the only information that you can get is the stuff that people put on the networks for other people to access. The terrible security problems you read about typically don't involve the Internet as much as they do the lack of computer security at certain businesses and government organizations.

People cannot get into your computer just because you are using the Net. The one thing you do have to protect while using the Net is the information that you send to someone else. It is possible, but highly unlikely, that someone could "grab" that information while it is flying down the Net to its destination. In other words, don't send extremely confidential messages.

If you do want to send totally secure messages, there is relatively simple software that you can use with other people to make your messages entirely private — so private, in fact, that if you lose the "key" to the code you won't be able to read your own mail. If security is an important issue to you, especially because of cross-cultural missionary work or the like, you should consider using encryption software at least for the more sensitive communication. Or you could just get your teenager to put the messages into teen-speak; surely no outsider could break that code!

Question 9: "Given all of the publicity about smut dealers on the computer networks, and even attempted child luring, is it safe for any children to be on?"

These are reasonable concerns. The Internet is sometimes compared to the wild frontier West, where there was considerable lawlessness. Stronger federal regulations are certainly increasing the criminality of using the Internet to exchange obscene materials and to lure children. But enforcing the laws is an entirely different matter; the Internet is vast and extremely difficult to regulate effectively. Let's not underestimate the sinfulness of people in this fallen world.

On the other hand, there is not nearly as much of this kind of material on the Internet as news reports would suggest. I spend hours on the Net every week, and I rarely run across any of it. To some extent you have to be looking for the worst material in order to find it. Frankly, it's probably easier for most people to get objectionable material from local magazine racks and public libraries than it is to get it on the Internet. As I explain in chapter six, you can keep your children from getting access to the vast majority of this kind of stuff simply by keeping them off what are called *newsgroups* (they really should be called "discussion groups"). Since you have to have special software to use newsgroups, the easiest thing for a parent to do is to control offspring access to this kind of software. Some surfers think that without the newsgroups the Net is not valuable. I've found mostly the opposite to be the case; newsgroups are not nearly as valuable as the information on the World Wide Web. Moreover, *mailing lists* (free e-mail "subscription" lists) can be better than newsgroups (I've listed dozens of the Christian mailing lists in the appendix).

Also, many of the major companies that provide consumer access to the Internet, along with other specialized companies, now provide software that parents can use to control their offspring's access to sections of the Internet, including particular newsgroups. I expect this kind of software to be widely used and highly valued by many parents, schools and libraries.

Question 10: "One of my friends tried for months to get hooked up to the Internet. He finally gave up in frustration. Is it really so hard to get on?"

Wow! I feel sorry for that chap. It took me and six computer-technician friends only about two weeks of full-time work to get my computer working on the Internet. And as soon as they left, the screen froze with the following message blinking in pink and green: "HA! TRY IT AGAIN, YOU COMPUTER DUMMY!" I was discouraged, to say the least.

Seriously, it's no longer so difficult to get hooked up to the Net. The stories you heard were probably true, but the growing consumer demand for Net access has created a host of alternatives for easy, virtually 5-minute hook-ups (assuming you have the necessary computer and modem, and you know how to use them). It is now almost as easy as getting telephone service to your home. Given my last experience with the phone company, I take that back; the Internet is easier. Chapter three explains your options for Internet access. The appendix provides specific information about finding an Internet access provider in your area.

Question 11: "I heard that e-mail addresses could be the Mark of the Beast (Rev. 19:20). What do you think?"

Now I'm receiving e-mail asking if e-mail is the Mark of the Beast! I wonder if these people are serious. I've heard that the Mark is social security numbers, universal product code (UPC) symbols and credit-card numbers (evil enough without being *the* mark). But the *Beast*?

One thing to consider is that if the Devil is using e-mail addresses he surely isn't very smart. People change their e-mail addresses, and frequently mail gets returned undeliverable. Satan is going to be totally confused if he calls the roll with e-mail addresses. Simply put, e-mail addresses are a confusing mess— nearly "virtual"chaos in cyberspace.

There really is not a lot of standardization in e-mail addresses. In the United States, Internet addresses usually end in things like "edu" (educational institution), "com" (company), "org" (non-profit organization) and "gov" (government). In other countries, the address ends with a code for the particular nation (such as "uk" for United Kingdom). Also, the commercial online services, such as CompuServe and America Online, use e-mail addresses that don't necessarily follow those rules; *all* of their addresses end in "com," regardless of whether the address is held by a person or organization.

In short, e-mail addresses are a messy proposition for the Mark of the Beast. I theorize that e-mail address *confusion* is more the work of the devil. People who have lost their computer files containing all of their friends' e-mail addresses have become violent and depressed. Another, very different, idea was suggested by one of my Net friends: e-mail address confusion is a reflection of the Tower of Babel, where God created communication problems so human beings couldn't generate quite as much evil together.

I don't know what to say about all of this with any certainty. I'll leave it to the theologians, who can send me e-mail suggestions at <schu@calvin.edu>, or is it <schu@gospelcom.net>? Oh well, good luck getting it to me.

Question 12: "I own a Christian business and considered selling my products on the Internet until someone told me that commerce is discouraged. Is that true?"

I'd like to know what kind of products you sell. Right now people are selling virtually everything on the Net, from coffee to underwear (excuse me, *undergarments*) to Bibles. I have yet to see things like Christian wallpaper or Christian pens and pencils being sold on the Net, although I've seen them displayed at the Christian Booksellers Convention.

Actually, I should say that folks are *trying* to sell these things on the Internet. No one knows how much actual buying takes place on the Net, but projections given by the big-wig observers of the Net suggest that Internet sales every year represent a larger percentage of the Gross National Product in the United States alone. And there are documented cases of some businesses selling millions of dollars worth of stuff on the Internet.

The Net is not a place where you can sell *anything* quickly and easily, in spite of what some of the popular publications seem to suggest. The most effective approaches to Net sales take into account the distinct culture of the Net — the mind-set and expectations of Net surfers. I talk about these at length in the last chapter of the book, providing specific suggestions for designing your personal Web pages or your organization's pages (computer generated pages that are read by Net surfers). Clearly the Web is becoming a major commercial medium, but Christian businesses have been much slower to get online.

I would encourage you to consider using the Net for sales. But be careful of *netiquette* — the established etiquette of Internet communication. Generally speaking, people expect commerce to be passive on the Internet (i.e., they expect customers to come to sellers). People can get very upset if they are sent unsolicited appeals for products and services.

Question 13: "I work for a large missions organization involved in international outreach. Is the Internet a reliable way for us to communicate with missionaries and nationals around the world?"

During the last several years, international access to the Net has improved enormously. Some of the large commercial online services such as CompuServe, as well as other, regional organizations, are providing excellent Internet access in most developed and many developing nations (see the appendix for information about finding international Internet access providers). In addition, some of the least-developed countries are creating wireless telephone systems to serve large regions that never had wire-based infrastructures. If some of the large Internet access providers do not have their own direct connections in the area in which you work, they likely have arrangements with other telephone companies to provide connections for them.

There are a couple of concerns, however. First, your e-mail and other Net traffic may not be particularly secure. Local and federal governments may monitor the messages sporadically, or at least to the best of their ability. In addition, it may not be legal for you to use encryption software to "code" your messages so government officials or others can't read them. Be sure to check on the regulations in your country by getting in touch with the governmental body responsible for communications regulation (see appendix).

But the overwhelmingly good news is that many thousands of missionaries will be able to access the Net fairly easily, dependably and securely. In fact, a friend and colleague of mine in Guatemala now has remarkably good Net access via some type of regional network. Given how poor the postal service is in that country, and how expensive regular telephone calls are, this Net access has been a real blessing for his work. I discuss missionary use of the Internet in chapter five.

Question 14: "Our pastor says that he was not taught anything about computers and the Internet in seminary. He also says that he can't imagine that computers could really help him pastor our church. Why should we help him get on the Internet?"

As I mentioned in the introduction to this book, seminary *students* are changing the face of seminary technology. Many seminarians use their own laptop computers right in the classroom. Quite a few of the faculty also use computers. Slowly but surely, divinity schools and seminaries are getting on the Net. It has taken quite a while, but seminaries are finally moving into the computer age.

There are many tasks that your pastor might not take care of more efficiently or effectively with computers. I would suggest, however, that pastoring can be assisted significantly by computers and the Internet. Pastors can conduct significant Net research in everything from scriptural interpretation to methods of evangelism and theology. In addition, pastors can commune online with other pastors, exchanging ideas and concerns, discussing sermon topics and sermon content, garnering material for sermons, following current cultural trends and phenomena, and so forth. They can also participate in denominational discussion groups and take advantage of online resources for church education. Finally, pastors can gain access to the same ministry resources that lay members might find helpful in their own devotional lives. These are just some of the potential benefits. I discuss others in chapter five, and I provide in the appendix many listings of online resources that will help your pastor.

I could suggest much more about general use of computers by pastors for things such as church management, but that is hardly within the scope of this book. In short, I would hope that you would reconsider your pastor's own assumptions about the value of computers and the Internet in parish ministry. My guess is that by the time your church is ready for its next pastor you will have some very different feelings about this topic. If you call a pastor right out of seminary, I can almost guarantee it.

Question 15: "I read recently that a group in Europe is predicting that the Internet will soon stop working because of all of the people using it. Why should Christians get involved in a medium that may come crashing down, anyway?"

I, too, have read these reports. The doomsayers seem to believe that the Net will "crash" because of the overload of new users. So what? Poor communication has never stopped the church before! The church throughout history has invested all kinds of money and time in projects that produced very little fruit. So what if no one is on the Internet? So what if the Net crashes? The church can talk to itself. Don't *you* like to hear yourself talking?

Seriously, I have read these kinds of apocalyptic warnings for the last few years. There will always be naysayers who generate publicity by announcing what amounts to apocalyptic prophecy about technology. For every naysayer there are just as many people who take the opposite view, namely, that the Net will solve all human problems. If the naysayers are too negative, the optimists are too positive, almost triumphalistic. All media seem to elicit these two, contrary responses — one that sees the new medium almost as the end of the world, and the other one that sees it as the salvation of the world. The truth is nearly always somewhere in between these two extremes, as I argue in chapter two.

Our task as Christians, I believe, is to claim every new medium for Christ. If a new medium comes along, we should use it. Of course, all of the tough questions are in the decisions about *how* to use it. Our fundamental message, the Gospel of Jesus Christ, never changes. But the means of communication do change, just as they have since Christ walked the earth. To say that the Internet is for Christians is another way of saying that it belongs to Jesus Christ, our God and our Lord — not to us.

I don't believe the Net will crash permanently. There is money to be made by building the Net at a faster rate than people are able to use it.

Send your questions for future editions of the book to me at the following e-mail address:

schu@gospelcom.net

Also, you can read answers to new questions on the World Wide Web before they are published in the next edition. Point your web browsers to the following URL (Web address):

http://www.gospelcom.net/ifc/

Thanks! Blessed surfing.

Quentin J. Schultze

CHAPTER TWO

Welcome to the "Inter-what?"

Is There Really an Internet?

One of the most popular words in Internet culture is "virtual." "Internetters" (I think I just invented that word) speak of "virtual community," "virtual government," "virtual office," and just about everything else as "virtual."

The idea is that computers create something that replicates or imitates reality, thereby creating a new reality. So the business person works at home, talking to clients on the phone and sending them messages via computer connections. This person's home is a "virtual office" — a place to conduct business, not a "real" office in an office complex or a corporate skyscraper.

> **"The Internet is 'virtual.' It dynamically imitates all kinds of other human activities, from conversation to business, education, fellowship and ministry."**

Some colleges and universities, for example, offer virtual courses via the Internet. Students never have to set foot on a geographic campus. They dial a telephone number, hook up their computers to that phone line, and send and receive papers, texts, grades, assignments, and all the rest. They can even "chat" with their instructors and "virtual classmates."

In one sense, then, it doesn't make an awful lot of sense to talk about "the Internet." Instead, we should discuss what people do *with* or *on* the Internet. The Net is just the means to a variety of ends, from education to politics (yep, politicians are now launching campaigns on the Internet, and some of them seem to think that the Net will usher in a new world of democratic government — a "mouse" in every pot, or was it a chicken in every computer?).

Think about it this way: neighborhoods are not just the buildings and roads, but all of the relationships, activities and events that occur in that neighborhood, as well as all of the people who live in the structures and traverse the streets. Similarly, the Internet is a culture of people (actually, many cultures) with particular values and beliefs, using computers and other technologies to communicate with one another for a host of reasons. Just as neighborhoods change, so does the Internet. Taking the analogy one step further, we could say that the Internet's "neighborhoods" change daily as people move in and out, as new structures are built, and as the roads are improved or ruined.

The Internet depends on computer technology for its existence. No computers, no Internet. When computers are *down* (not working), the Internet evaporates. My brother in Minneapolis says that in Minnesota there are two seasons: winter and road construction. On the Internet there are two seasons: *up* computers and *down* computers.

Estimates put the number of *new* Internet users at about 300,000 monthly — more than the residents of my city, Grand Rapids, Michigan. Who knows if those numbers are really accurate, since there's no way to measure precisely. Certainly the numbers are growing. This incredible influx of people changes the "virtual" Internet every day. It's like whole towns and cities moving from one place to another, or like thousands of people joining ongoing discussions, or like new suburbs being constructed overnight. In the case of the Internet, however, no one can actually see all of these people "moving" along the highways, because on the Net they are "virtual people."

> **"The Internet provides a means for people to replace various kinds of *transportation* with new forms of communication."**

On the Internet one doesn't have to send a "physical" message (a letter, for instance, which on the Net they call *snail mail*) to a friend. Instead, you can send them an "electronic message" (also known as "email" or "e-mail" or "E-mail"). You don't need a horse, a car or even a letter carrier. All you need is your computer and at least one more computer on the other end of the line, as well as a medium for the message to travel. The major media used are telephone lines, coaxial cables (like cable-TV cables), fiber-optic "cables" and satellite transmitters.

The Internet is one means of communication—one medium. The Net includes the people who do the communicating, the technologies they use, and all of the values and beliefs that shape how and why the people communicate. If this is still a blur, don't give up. The next section puts it all together.

What's the Infosuperhighway?

Whoever invented this term should be examined by linguists and other experts. It's a confusing concept that has cast the entire Internet phenomenon in a cloud of confusion and hype. I'll give you a realistic and honest assessment of the concept.

Somewhere, somehow, someone got the idea that someday soon huge, all-powerful media would effortlessly pump messages into peoples' homes all day and night. The most frequently used example is the "promise" of 500-channel TV. Suddenly the news media were trumpeting the great benefits of this "information superhighway."

It reminds me of the myth that everyone will be able to fly from one place to another using personal flying machines that strap to the backs of fearless navigators like you and me (well, maybe like you). I enjoyed seeing this kind of contraption depicted with special effects in the movie *The Rocketeer*. Are we all really going to start flying around? Of course not. But such high-tech myths are very appealing.

In my more cynical moments I think that the infosuperhighway myth was foisted on the public by the entertainment and telephone industries. Together these organizations, along with the computer industry, stand to gain the most from the deregulation of telecommunications. One popular term these days is *convergence* — the merging of the entertainment, telephone and computer industries. In recent years Wall Street has witnessed buyout mania among some of these industries. But corporate alliances alone will not usher in the mythical infosuperhighway of 500-channel TV.

This is the kind of nonsensical hype that has been attached to the largely meaningless term "infosuperhighway." Somehow this highway, whatever it is, will improve government, education, parenting, entertainment — on and on. Forget the hoopla. People are sinners. The highway was not built by God, but by fallen human beings. There will never be a boundless medium that *automatically* injects truth and justice into the world. No medium will be any better than the people who run it and the practical limits of human communication under the shadow of the Fall.

> **"The Internet is not the *publicized* infosuperhighway. In fact, there really is no such thing as an infosuperhighway as reporters depict it."**

Who cares about 500-channel TV? Most of us watch only a few channels, anyway. As my colleague, Robert Fortner, has argued, there will probably never be any "universal" communication service available equally to all people. I think he's right. Forget the hype!

The Internet promises *potentially* beneficial communication, but certainly not perfect communication. In spite of all of the worthwhile uses of the Internet, there are all kinds of evil uses. Let's not let the hype get in the way of reality.

So What *Is* the Internet, Anyway?

Now we're ready to get to the heart of the Internet:

> **"The Internet is a "digital" network that makes it possible for people to communicate from computer to computer."**

That's it. Now you know what to say at lunch or dinner to impress your friends: "Did you know that, technologically speaking, the Internet is a digital network?," or, "Did you know that the Net allows people to communicate between computers?" Say it to yourself a few times before you forget it. This is the reality behind the hoopla.

The interesting thing is *what* we can communicate from one computer to another. Theoretically speaking, we could communicate any of the following:

- **any text** (i.e., any written or printed words, such as a book or letter)

- **any sound** (e.g., a musical recording or a conversation)

- **any image** (i.e., any still or moving image, such as photographs and videos)

Now you've got a glimpse of the "revolutionary" nature of the Internet. Any text, sound, and image potentially can be put in a *digital* (i.e., computerized) form and transmitted from one computer to another.

All of this would not be so significant except for the fact that the Internet is being connected to thousands of homes and offices every day. At my home, for instance, our daughter has been sending e-mail back and forth with a friend in Japan. It takes a few seconds to send a letter, and there's no direct charge. Our son not only communicates with friends, but he *surfs* the Internet in search of information for school papers, personal hobbies (including musical groups), ministry (he is one of the youth leaders at church), and computers. My wife organizes via our home computer an electronic mailing "list" of former classmates from her high school graduating class, sending them updates about what's happening in their lives.

I also use the Net for a host of activities. I read daily newspapers and weekly and monthly magazines *on* my computer. I communicate with colleagues who reside all over the world. I preview movies by connecting to computers that store the publicity releases and "trailers" for new releases. I follow the text (typed on keyboards) conversations of various groups of people who discuss what's happening with the Internet. I send manuscripts to book and periodical publishers. I sample newly released songs from various Christian artists, such as Charlie Peacock, who has been a leader in Internet use among Christian musicians, writers and producers. I read the latest theological "findings" published at seminaries and debate theological issues with laity and clergy alike. I read on my computer the public computer files of various religious cults to see what they believe and advocate. And all of this is just the tip of the digital iceberg.

"The Internet is often called 'the network of computer networks.' Unlike the mythical infosuperhighway, it's a real network of tens of thousands of computer networks and perhaps 40 million individuals all over the world."

Any person or organization that taps into that network with their own computer is suddenly in the middle of the digital revolution in communication — the revolution that enables many people to transmit and receive text, sound and image. A computer "network" is simply a group of computers connected through a medium to enable people to send and receive digital "information."

If the infosuperhighway is a myth, the Internet is the reality. Unlike the ideal image of perfect communication, the Internet is a network filled with godly and godless messages. A few of the messages bounce around various networks and computers but never find their destination — they get lost in *cyberspace,* the collective computerized networks of telephone lines, coaxial cable (like cable-TV wire), satellites, cellular phones and more. Other messages zip swiftly from a sleek, laptop computer in corporate Taiwan to bulky desktop computers in Mexican schools. The Internet is everything from wonderful daily devotionals to repugnant smut, popular magazines to university courses, love letters to hate mail, all communicated from computer to computer.

Who's in Charge of the Internet?

For all practical purposes, no one is in charge of the Internet. There are self-regulatory groups that hammer out technical rules for how computers should be connected. There are some governments that try to regulate message flow (called *traffic*), but not always successfully. There are unspoken rules or network etiquette (sometimes called *netiquette*) that most users try to follow (such as don't send an advertisement to someone who hasn't requested it) — again, not always successfully.

Some people compare the Internet to the Western frontier of the United States; they even celebrate the "lawlessness" and apparent personal freedom. But with such freedom comes abuse. We read of attempts by some Internet users to transmit child pornography or even to lure kids away from home. The Internet is all of this hope and dismay, and more. For the time being, the Internet is a remarkably unregulated medium that can really excite and infuriate just about anyone.

"One result of the lack of net regulation is the illusion of a completely free ride."

I regularly hear from people who say that postage is expensive but the Internet is "free." Well, it seems like it's free to many users simply because no one is directly in charge of collecting tariffs or tolls from every user. Much of the communicating via the Internet is subsidized by the organizations that make the computers available to users. Businesses, for instance, are hooking up to the Internet in droves, but few of them tell their employees what it costs for such connections — easily thousands of dollars a year. Meanwhile, these employees use lunchtime and evenings to send personal messages or download games or evangelize on the Net. The same sense of "free" usage is true of colleges and universities, where faculty and students now take things like e-mail for granted until the campus computer network goes down.

Since no one is collecting tolls from all individual users, some Internet aficionados tend to think that everything should be "free." Although this lack of direct charge is indeed true today, the Net will clearly not always be such a free ride. For one thing, advertisements are starting to pop up all over the Net. Some online periodicals and directories, for instance, display ad images and copy. Someone is paying for these ads, even if it isn't the individual Internet users. In addition, there is a growing tendency among some of the so-called "information providers" (i.e., organizations that supply information on their computers for others to read, hear or see) to charge for information. *The Wall Street Journal,* for instance, has charged a subscription fee for access to its Internet version.

But the most obvious charges, as we shall see, are for users to connect to the Internet. Some cities have "free nets" that let residents connect without charge via local telephone lines; usually these lines are fairly limited, enabling only a few people at a time to get on the Net from that location. Most individuals who want to get on the Internet from their homes will simply have to pay an organization to get connected, whether via a telephone line, coaxial cable, satellite, fiber optic (thin glass "wires" that transmit digital signals by light), cellular telephone, etc. Moreover, organizations that provide "free" Internet connections to their users, such as the connection that schools supply for students, are collecting those fees from tuition or other indirect charges.

Historically speaking, the Internet was created and developed primarily on federal subsidies from the United States. Some of these funds were educational, and others were tied more specifically to various kinds of scientific research, including military-related research. During the 1960s and '70s, however, the general public knew little or nothing about what was eventually called *the Internet.*

As the cost of personal computers decreased, and the network of computer networks expanded, the Internet was no longer merely a scientific or educational endeavor. But the old mind-set that relied on public subsidies and no regulation has continued to shape many peoples' perceptions of the Net. The magazines read by Internetphiles decry both commercialization and direct fees for personal Internet connections, while championing complete freedom of expression. Unfortunately, this type of attitude ignores the fact that public resources of all kinds are limited these days. There is no free ride. Moreover, if the governments don't regulate the Net, others will shape net content indirectly through financial influence.

> **"Commercialization of the Internet is inevitable. Like radio and television before it, the Net will have to find ways of paying for its growing menu of information and entertainment."**

Some of these costs will be passed along to you and me as users. In addition, many costs will be passed on to advertisers. Let's hope that advertisers will use their money wisely and in a stewardly fashion. Let's also hope that Christian ministries will not commercialize themselves on the Internet the way some of them have in broadcasting, with endless barrages of fund-raising gimmicks and lamentable slips into self-help techniques masquerading as the Gospel of Jesus Christ.

Finally, I can't help but believe that thorough enforcement of any regulation of the Internet will never be possible. Certainly the Net will be increasingly centralized and standardized — more like a booming metropolis than a free-wheeling frontier. But computer-to-computer communication is not as easily controlled and monitored as broadcasting. Along with centralization will come decentralization in the form of all kinds of new computer networks that are hooked up (on the Net they say *wired*) to the Internet. In addition, individuals and groups will increasingly use various kinds of *encryption* to make their private messages inaccessible to people who don't have the necessary passwords or encryption *keys.*

Are Commercial "Online" Services Like America Online and CompuServe Part of the Internet?

During recent years, while the Internet was growing enormously, a number of companies began creating their own, commercial versions of the Net. Instead of first hooking up directly to the Internet, which at that time was highly non-commercial, they built huge computer systems connected to telephone lines all over the United States and increasingly the world. By calling a local telephone number, people could connect their own computers to the service's big computers, thereby retrieving information from the services' computers as well as exchanging e-mail via the services' computers.

These *commercial online services,* such as CompuServe, Delphi, GEnie, Prodigy, America Online, eWorld and others, made it easier and less expensive than the Internet for business and individuals to use digital communication. E-mail, probably more than anything else, fueled the growth of these services. In time, the commercial online services figured out how to connect their computer systems to the Internet, thereby letting their subscribers exchange messages with people on the Net. It took several years, but eventually most of the services were able to make themselves more or less fully compatible with the Internet, so they, in effect, became part of the Internet.

E-mail was not the only attraction of the commercial online services. The services' computers included all kinds of information, including periodicals, the kinds of reference materials available in libraries and on CD-ROMs, "places" for users to *chat* ("talk," using their computer keyboards to type messages) with other users, software to *download* (transfer from another computer to your own) free and for charge, catalogs of products for sale, and on and on. All of this kind of stuff is available at a fairly nominal monthly charge (less than $10 U.S.), although there are often additional charges for special information (such as searches of back issues of periodicals) and for spending a lot of time hooked up to the service's computers.

"In the last few years it's become increasingly clear that the Internet will permanently dwarf commercial online services like America Online and CompuServe."

The Internet has tens of millions of users, whereas even the biggest online services, such as CompuServe and America Online, have only a few million users. More than that, there is so much more to "do" on the Internet (as you'll soon see) that the online services by contrast look rather digitally anemic.

Consequently, CompuServe and the other online services are increasingly in the business of providing access to the Internet, not just selling access to their own computer services. I'll go so far as to say that their future depends largely on how well they tap the rapidly growing public demand for Internet access, especially the *World Wide Web,* a fun, user-friendly way of "travelling" around the Net. Because most of these online services have customer-support staffs, the necessary software, and especially because they have local telephone hook-ups (*dial-ups*) in many areas, they have moved quickly towards the business of providing Internet connections for their own subscribers.

The individual subscriber to an online service typically is able to access either the service's own computers full of information and entertainment or the Internet itself — the network of networks. However, it is not clear that these online services will make it easy for people to travel the other way — from the Internet to the online services — certainly not without an additional fee. So there will likely continue to be some kinds of digital messages (text, audio and image) that you will be able to get only by subscribing to one of these services (the appendix includes a short description and assessment of the major online services).

I'm no prophet, but in the long run I don't see a bright future for the online services unless they make some significant changes. As it becomes easier and cheaper for people to connect directly to the Internet, demand will decrease for such proprietary operations with rather limited "content."

The future of online services rests in:

1. Their ability to provide Internet access to their own subscribers,

2. Their ability to provide specialized, highly valued information unavailable on the Net,

3. Their ability to provide special, highly useful and user-friendly directories and search tools for their subscribers to use on the Internet, and

4. Their ability to provide international Net access, since both national economies and personal relationships are becoming increasingly global.

"Inter-what?"

The Internet, then, is a network of computer networks. Individuals can "tap" into that network, using it for everything from entertainment to education and ministry. Most people first get on the Internet to exchange e-mail with family, friends and colleagues. Soon they find out that the Net includes not only text, but sound and images as well. While the infosuperhighway is largely a myth, the Internet is a reality. The biggest attraction to the Net is now the World Wide Web, which requires no special technical expertise and is fun to use. Commercial online services like CompuServe provide easy, relatively inexpensive access to the Web in North America and increasingly the rest of the world. So do long-distance and, increasingly, local telephone companies. Cable TV companies are also part of the business of Net access.

CHAPTER THREE

Getting on the Internet

Believe me, the hardest thing for most new Internet users used to be getting on the Net, not using the network once they had connected to it. I've heard from people who have spent literally weeks monkeying around with their computer and software to get hooked up to the network of networks. My heart goes out to all people who have wasted such time in frustration and sometimes even anger. Fortunately, those days are rapidly coming to a close.

This chapter tells you what you need to know to get hooked up to the Internet. It also recommends some of the easy ways of doing it. Fortunately, some of the easier ways are also relatively inexpensive. Relax and "listen up." Before you can get on, you've got to make sure that your computer equipment is capable of making the connection.

What Equipment Do I Need to Get on the Internet?

Simple: a degree in computer science, $10,000 dollars, an Internet "geek" friend and stock in one of the telecommunications conglomerates. JUST KIDDING!

1. A computer

First, you need an adequate computer, either a Macintosh or a PC (PCs — personal computers — were formerly known as "IBM compatibles," even though there are now Macintosh compatibles; *compatible* means simply more than one manufacturer or brand of a particular kind of computer that uses the same kind of software). If you don't have a computer, don't run out and indiscriminately spend a bunch of cash to get one. Go to a reliable local computer store and tell them what you will do with the computer *besides* get on the Internet, such as word processing (writing), games, office accounting, etc. Get a computer that will do *those* things; the same one will almost certainly take care of your Internet needs.

I won't get into any of the endless debates about which is better, a Mac or a PC. But I will say this: If you get a PC, be sure it will effortlessly and quickly run the latest versions of software. I use primarily Macs because our children learned to use this kind of system in school. Also, I do quite a bit of high-quality graphics work, which I find easier on a Mac.

If you buy a used computer, ask the same questions: Will it run the current kinds of software that will enable you to do whatever you need to do with the computer? If not, don't get it. Some people may tell you that you can easily "upgrade" the older system to make it work, but this option is usually not worth the expense and effort; worse yet, sometimes these upgrades don't work very well.

"Get a computer that is one notch below the current state of the art."

There is rarely a need to buy the latest, fastest, hottest computer. Instead, buy one that is one notch lower. This will generally save you quite a bit of money and will give you a solid, well-tested computer system. If you can find a used one, great, but they're not so easy to locate at a good price.

2. A modem

Second, you'll need a modem. This is just a device that hooks between your computer and your telephone line, enabling your computer to exchange messages with other computers connected directly or indirectly to that phone line.

The good news is that most new computers these days come with modems built in. The bad news is that some of those modems don't permit speedy transfer of messages over the phone line. You don't want a slow modem.

Get the fastest modem you can afford, but not slower than what's commonly referred to as a "28.8 bps" modem (this signifies how fast the messages travel through the modem; the higher the number, the faster the speed).

I prefer to use *external* modems (i.e., modems that are not inside the computer) because they can be replaced more easily when the costs come down on faster ones. But if you have or are buying a small, laptop computer to carry around, you'll probably want an internal modem. In any case, get a modem that is compatible with your computer (e.g., don't get one designed to be used with a Mac if you own a PC). For $100 you should be able to get a very satisfactory new modem.

Incidentally, as the cable-TV companies start offering Internet hook-ups to their coaxial cables, and as satellite companies increasingly offer Internet access, the telephone modem will be only one of many ways of connecting to the Internet. The cable-TV companies will provide special, high-speed modems. In addition, many businesses and a few homes already use *digital* phone lines that require special devices similar to modems. For the time being, you needn't concern yourself with these kinds of devices.

How Do I Get my Computer & Modem Connected to the Internet?

You've got a computer and a compatible modem, but you now need to connect to the Internet. Organizations that provide these connections are commonly known as *Internet service providers or ISPs.*

> **"The Internet providers are like telephone companies except that they don't have to bring the wire to your house; it's already there."**

You'll see more and more local and long-distance phone companies offering to connect you to the Internet. They use existing telephone wires and other kinds of cables, or in some cases satellites, to connect you to the Internet. Think of an Internet service provider as a long-distance phone company that connects you to other computers all over the world, instead of merely to telephones all over the world. The big difference, however, is that in some parts of the world you don't normally have to pay "per-call" or, in Internet lingo, per message *packet.*

Ask some friends who use the Internet how they got connected.

Find out how much it costs them (usually $20 or so monthly for unlimited use). In the appendix, I list some of the big providers that have connections in many cities. But there are many local and especially regional providers that do an excellent job. Some of them have special family plans or nighttime use plans, and so forth. If you can, shop around a bit to see what's available. Try the telephone book under "Internet" or "telecommunications." Also call a few local organizations that probably have Internet connections, such as colleges and universities as well as larger corporations. Ask for the person who handles the computer system and request information about the organization that supplies their Internet access. If you have the Internet at your office, ask the computer people who provides the service. Call a local computer store (a real computer store, not just an appliance place that sells a few computers) and ask them about local Internet access providers. Finally, check out the advertisements in computer magazines. You'll find all kinds of ads for Net access, and if you buy a magazine you might even get free Net software with the periodical.

"If you are a member of a denomination, check to see if you can get access to the Net through any denominational or cross-denominational networks."

A growing number of churches are providing access to the Net as well as to denominational news and discussion services. The Lutheran Church—Missouri Synod, for instance, has an extensive network with Internet connections for e-mail. Many mainline church groups are involved in EcuNet (see appendix). Presbyterians have PresbyNet. Roman Catholics and the Southern Baptist Convention have areas on CompuServe.

If you have friends locally or in another city who are on the Internet, they can get a list of local providers for you from the Net. It is not difficult to find a provider; this is a rapidly growing, increasingly competitive industry. I give specific information on this in the appendix.

Another option is to sign up with one of the online services like Prodigy, America Online and CompuServe. In addition to providing their own information services just for their subscribers, they now provide essentially complete and relatively easy access to the Internet. It's an easy process of calling their toll-free number (see appendix) to have the membership materials sent directly to your home. Within a few days you'll be online.

"In some cities there are "free-nets" that connect users to the Internet more or less free of charge."

Free-nets are non-profit organizations that provide free Net access in communities. Free-nets are a great idea, but unfortunately they rarely have enough incoming phone lines to keep users happy; you can call for hours trying to get an open (not busy) line to use to connect to the Internet. If you have friends locally who are already on the Net, they can probably give you information about any area free-nets (see appendix).

If you are even a part-time college or university student, you've probably got Internet access that you didn't even know about. Most of these schools provide easy access for students and faculty, including phone numbers for off-campus access and special computers already connected for on-campus access to the Net.

Yet another option is a long-distance phone company, such as MCI, Sprint and AT&T. If you use one of these companies for your phone service, you could call them to see what kind of price they would give on Internet access. Their services can be a good deal, especially for people who travel a lot, since their service is available increasingly around the world from just about any phone.

Soon many areas of the United States will have Internet connections provided by the cable-TV companies. It's too early to know how well these will work, but technically they could be very fast and dependable. Stay tuned in your area, especially if you already have a cable-TV subscription. No doubt the company will send you information with your bill.

Finally, most medium-sized cities and larger have at least one major local computer *bulletin board service* (BBS) that offers at least e-mail access to the Internet. BBSs are like mini-online services at the local level, with some connections to other computer networks, including the Internet. Most of these charge for the service, and the service is not normally as good as that provided by Internet providers, long-distance phone companies or the major online services such as CompuServe. But it might be the least expensive route to go in your area. Just ask a few of your computer friends about local BBSs, and they can probably tell you who to contact.

Here's what to look for in an Internet provider:

1. Reliable service, not busy signals or "crashes" that suddenly hang up your modem.

2. Reasonable cost, usually $20 or less monthly.

3. Customer support, so you have someone to help you when you have a problem (customer support is often the best reason to use a local provider).

4. A connection speed that is no slower than your modem's maximum speed, and preferably faster.

5. Related services, such as the opportunity to publish some of your material on the Internet free of charge by putting it on your Internet provider's computer *server* (a computer called a Net server because it "serves" information to other computers).

6. The full complement of Internet services, including e-mail and especially the World Wide Web (just make sure the provider has *PPP* service; this will give you all you need).

7. Software to use to get on the Net easily and inexpensively (a good provider should be able to give you the software disks ready to be installed in your computer; more on this in the next section).

8. The software for subscribers to use to "filter" or "block" pornographic or other offensive newsgroups and Web sites.

Don't be intimidated by the fact that you might have to call up a few schools, stores or friends to find out about Internet providers. Before you know it, you'll probably meet someone that will help you get connected!

What Software Do I Need to Get on the Internet?

Software is the stuff that enables your computer to do what you'd like it to — like an internal computer map that gives the computer directions. The software you'll need depends on what you want to do on the Net. There are different softwares for different types of communication. But the good news is that there is free software to do just about anything you'd like to do. I recommend that you get two kinds of software: one to use e-mail and the other to get on the Web. Don't worry about all of the other bells and whistles, such as *FTP* (file transfer protocol—a way of transferring files of information from one computer to another), *telnet* and *newsgroup* software. The average user simply doesn't need this software.

"In most cases your Internet provider will give you the software you need to use their connection."

The online companies like CompuServe do this, as do the larger and many of the smaller Internet access providers. If you're a student, you can probably retrieve copies of free software right off of the school computer system. Most new computers today come *bundled* with the necessary software. Internet-savvy friends can give you copies.

I would recommend starting with only two types of software: one for e-mail (such as Eudora), and one for surfing the World Wide Web (such as Netscape Navigator or Microsoft Explorer). You may also need the software to make the connection with your Internet provider (these are TCP and PPP softwares — letters that simply refer to the way that your computer will be able to connect with the Internet). This software is increasingly supplied with new computers, however. Here's a quick overview of the two kinds of software you'll want:

E-mail

An e-mail program will enable you to send letters back and forth with friends, colleagues and acquaintances on the Internet. It will also make it possible for you to subscribe to free mailing *lists,* which people use to share information, discuss issues and generally communicate about matters of common interest. Some of these are private, intra-organizational lists, while others are completely public. In the appendix, you'll find a listing of many of the Christian lists along with information about how to subscribe to them.

World Wide Web "Browser"

This state-of-the-art software let's you surf (travel) much of the Net by simply clicking your computer mouse on icons (images) and *hypertext* (specially marked words and phrases that automatically connect you to more info at other places).

Internet Connection Essentials

It is not difficult to get on the Internet. You'll need a computer, a modem, an Internet provider and some software. Be sure that you get both an e-mail connection and a connection to the World Wide Web. And don't forget to help a few others get online once you've made the connection.

Okay, you've got a computer and modem, you've signed up with an Internet provider, worked out any bugs with their customer support people, and you've got the software to do e-mail and the Web. Now you're ready for action!

CHAPTER FOUR

Finding People, Places and Resources on the Internet

M y wife, a home-health nurse, travels from house-to-house and apartment-to-apartment, providing nursing care primarily to older citizens. It's a rewarding vocation, and she loves the work. But it can also be an intimidating profession because of the wide array of medical situations she has to address without forewarning.

One day at dinner, she mentioned that she needed the latest information on Hepatitis C. After we finished eating, she perused the standard medical textbooks to find out more about the virus. Soon it was evident that the books wouldn't help; she needed recent information, the latest findings. She said to me somewhat skeptically, "Can you get medical information on your computer?" It was the kind of challenge I had been waiting for — a chance to prove the value of the Net to a skeptical spouse.

Within minutes we were cruising around the Internet, browsing gobs of information stored in computers around the world. It took perhaps fifteen minutes before we found exactly what she was looking for. At a medical school in the Eastern United States, a professor had created a site that reviewed the current literature on Hepatitis C, including the results of ongoing studies of treatment. Apparently the site was used primarily as a kind of virtual encyclopedia for medical students.

I have nearly always been able to find any information I needed on the Internet. I am not a novice at the Internet. Nevertheless, it is now possible especially via the Internet's World Wide Web for nearly anyone to conduct relatively comprehensive searches for people, places and resources. This chapter focuses on how to do this. Since the specific software or techniques change on the Net, I'm looking at the *approaches* to take. These approaches will not change as quickly as the particular *vehicles* (Internet lingo for specific software, databases and directories).

The most helpful information you can have is the actual address of the person or pages you seek. In e-mail lingo we speak of addresses (more below on this topic). On the Web people speak as much of *URLs* as addresses; a Web URL (uniform resource locator) is simply the address for a page. If you run across the URL in a magazine or an ad or on someone's business card, you can tell it is specifically for the Web because it contains the following beginning: *http://www* (the "http" is for "hypertext transfer protocol," the "www" is for "world wide web"). Once you're connected to the Web, and you've got the URL, all you have to do is type it in the proper "go to" or "open location" box in your Web browser, and it will take you there automatically (actually, on the Web your computer "contacts" another computer, which then sends the requested pages to your computer, typically in a few seconds; the data or images are then *yours,* on your computer).

How is the Internet's Info Organized?

How is the Net *organized?* Very poorly! There was never a grand plan or even a benevolent dictator to pull things together in a reasonably coherent fashion. The Net is organized more by the people who use it than it is by any external scheme, whether encyclopedias or almanacs.

"The Internet is best compared with a huge flea market, except that most of the stuff is free."

No one dictates how content will be organized on the Net any more than any individual can control how people display their wares at a flea market. Instead, every person and organization more or less creates their own method of displaying and organizing material. This is why surfing the Internet is often so appealing to people; they never know what they'll find at the Internet market, and anticipation makes the serendipitous searching a lot of fun.

But for those of us who don't have a lot of time for surfing, the

Net is primarily a source of information rather than entertainment. Some of the information comes from people we meet on the Net, and some of it comes from our own searches. Until someone fully indexes and organizes the Net — an unlikely proposition considering the "virtual" character of computer networks — searching the Net will be both a technical skill and an intuitive art. Experience helps, of course, and we can gain such experience both by our own efforts and by sharing it with each other. Online directories are helpful, but there will always be information that is not listed in directories.

A word to the wise here: the Net directories or "yellow pages" that you find in bookstores are always horribly out of date because the Net changes so rapidly. I provide a directory in the appendix to this book, but I would not pretend that it is completely accurate or comprehensive. The best directories are on the Net, where they can be updated daily, if necessary. The appendix to this book is updated for your use at the Gospel Communications Network (http://www.gospelcom.net/ifc/virtual.html). Drop by to say "hi" when you get on the Web.

"The Web, in particular, is easy to use once you understand its internal logic (some would say illogic)."

Every "place" on the Web is called a page, even if it is more than one page long. The first page at any site is usually called the home page. The best home pages should tell you what else is at that particular site, but a surprising number of them don't. If you already have a Web site address (URL, remember?), you don't have to go through any other pages to get to that page; you can go directly to any page for which you have an address (URL) and for which you have, if necessary, a password. "Web," then, is an appropriate term, because there are multiple ways of getting to a particular page at a particular site.

Anyone who has a page on the Web can link that page to other pages anywhere on the Web. For example, if I have a home page and I want others to know about the Gospel Communications Network, I can put GCN's address on my home page; anyone coming to my home page can then go directly to the GCN home page. In fact, the GCN address can be hidden "behind" a graphic or can be put on my page as a *hypertext* — colored text that automatically transfers the user to the address when the user clicks their mouse's cursor on that text (to see what hypertext looks like, look at the underlined, colored words on the back of the book). The Web is loaded with such graphic and hypertext links. Using these links, you can surf from one location to another without even knowing the specific addresses of the places you're visiting. This is one of the reasons why the Web is so user-friendly.

"In the broadest possible terms, the Web is organized around four concepts: subject, geography, institution and person."

---

1. Subject Organization

Subject organization is the most easily used and widely available means of finding information. The Web, in particular, has some extremely helpful subject directories, including Yahoo and InfoSeek (see appendix). But there are hundreds, perhaps even thousands of directories. Each of these is organized more or less like a "tree," with the broader categories listed first, followed by successively narrower, focused categories—all listed like menu items at a restaurant. "Health," for instance, might be listed before "disease," followed by "virus" and then "hepatitis." A particular Christian missionary organization in Africa might be listed under the following kinds of subjects in such a menu tree, with each word or phrase a hypertext link to the next one:

Society and Culture
Religion
Christianity
Organizations
Missions
Africa
(Name of organization)

When my wife and I searched for information on Hepatitis C, we soon discovered that the subject was nearly always listed under "diseases." In fact, every other key subject that we tried, such as "virus," did not work well. Once we discovered how the medical subject trees were generally organized, we located information on Hepatitis C at several different sites.

2. Geographical Organization

Geographical organization is much trickier to use, but it can find information that might not be found any other way. The basic principle is that the information you seek is likely to be located somewhere in particular, such as at a particular library, a specific seminary, a known publishing house, an identifiable ministry. If you know the geographical location of the place or person, often you can zero in on that place to see if what you are looking for is indeed located there. Geographical directories are similar to subject ones in the sense that they start broad (e.g., a continent or country), and get progressively specific (e.g., a state or city or region).

> **"On the Web, people speak of a person or organization's home page — the electronic or virtual home, not necessarily the geographic home."**

The problem with geographic location is that computer networks can easily put one person's or organization's information on a computer that is continents away from the same person's or organization's geographic home. The home page is actually anchored by computer, not by geography. In other words, an Internet "home" is practically anywhere one would like it to be, as long as there is a computer there that can "serve" the information to those who request it.

Weeks after my wife and I had found the information on Hepatitis C, my father-in-law was at our home, listening to me babble about the Web. I gave him a challenge: "Give me *any* topic or public person you would like to know about." "Okay," he said, "how about Hungary." Well, that was too easy a challenge, so I raised the stakes a bit: "How about a city or organization in Hungary?" He took the bait, giving me the name of a Hungarian city that he and my mother-in-law had visited while volunteering for mission work in the country.

Using a geographical search directory, I connected via the Internet to a computer in Hungary and located a listing for the city he mentioned. Within a few seconds an image was scanning onto my computer screen: a photo of the very church in which my in-laws had worshiped while in Hungary! "I know the pastor of that church!," my father-in-law exclaimed. He was impressed. I was lucky. Geographical searches are notoriously difficult.

3. Institutional Organization

Much of the Web is made up of a series of pages all listed under the home page of one institution. Colleges and universities, for example, typically have their own web pages, as do most major computer companies, non-profit organizations, governmental bodies and the like. The organization's computer can be located just about anywhere — it doesn't have to be at the geographical site of the institution. But the institution decides to have a collective presence on the Web, so instead of simply letting its various departments and employees create all kinds of Web pages at different sites, it puts them all under one, main address or home page on one computer.

"Searching for institutions on the Web is relatively easy because they tend to be included in directories and in the various search vehicles."

I have found, however, that typically one doesn't even need to search for an organization if you know how the addresses are usually constructed. Large U.S. corporations, in particular, have their own, obvious addresses ending in "com." Once you're on the Web, try going to a couple of corporate sites by creating the standard URL and adding the name of the organization for the *domain name* (believe it or not, the *computer name for the company*) as follows: http://www.*corporation*.com (don't include any final period or any quotation marks in the addresses I give in the text of the book). After you've tried a few corporate names in that kind of address, do the same for U.S. government sites, ending in "gov" instead of "com." If it's a long name, try an abbreviation, too, such as this: http://www.nasa.gov.

Ministries have not yet developed web sites to the extent of governments and corporations. And it's likely that ministries will often have a longer address that designates they are part of a group or network of groups instead of merely a free-standing site. In my judgment, this is a particularly good idea since it will produce more traffic at those sites for all ministries. As with e-mail, non-profit organizations' addresses on the Web in the U.S. normally end in "org" or, in a few cases, "net," which suggests a "network" or group of organizations instead of just one organization. Again, regardless of the precise address or location, institutions are relatively easy to access through directories and searches. Just remember to search "beneath" the home page of an organization once you get linked there (use the hypertext links on the home page); often there will be organizations "within" organizations because of the nature of the Web. Perhaps this will help Christian groups be more cooperative and less competitive — implicitly or explicitly.

"I expect many new alliances and networks of Christian organizations resulting from the value of working together on the Internet."

---

4. Personal Organization

Personal organization is the way that many Net users organize Web content according to their own interests and needs. Perhaps a good analogy is the way individuals organize their personal libraries in homes and offices. The difference is that the Web enables individuals to "reorganize" other peoples "pages" according to their own whims by creating their own directories or cataloging schemes.

Personal organization of information is a mark of electronic publishing, in general, and the Internet, in particular. Because it is so relatively easy and inexpensive to publish something on computer, especially compared with paper, the Internet has bred thousands of cottage publishing industries.

"In fact, just about anyone with a bit of time and access to a computer can publish their own novels, magazines, Bible commentaries, diatribes and the like on the Net."

Some people say that the Web is the "great leveller of publishing," putting everyone on equal ground, from a big publishing house to the average individual. This is not entirely true, since it takes some resources — time and money — to publish even on the Web. Nevertheless, the Web levels the publishing playing field enough that small, creative groups, for instance, can jump ahead of large organizations that get bogged down in organizational politics or short-term publishing paralysis. Also, some estimates suggest that Web publishing costs about one-thousandth of the cost of paper publishing, when you take into account all of the expenses of printing, paper, distribution, and so forth. This is one of the reasons that so many newspapers are beginning to publish on the Net.

"The Web has spawned all kinds of *personal home pages* that organize Internet content according to one individual's own interests, desires, hobbies, professional specialties, theological quirks, denominational ties, personal friendships, and so forth."

As odd as it may seem, these personal pages can be among the most valuable finds on the Web. Each one of them, in effect, is someone's attempt to organize the Web's chaos according to their own interests. Most of them admittedly are kind of silly and poorly constructed. But some of the best personal pages are as good as anything put on the Web by multinational corporations!

Suppose, for example, you're interested in Christians who are involved in professional or collegiate sports. If there were not a subject or organizational guide to Web resources, you just might find one on someone's own home page. In fact, I've found several of them; neither one was even remotely comprehensive, but they did provide excellent places to start the search. If I followed up those two findings with a fairly comprehensive search of the Web for other, related material, I could start my own, more comprehensive directory of Christians in sports.

You would not believe the number of personal home pages that provide this kind of uncataloged, largely unknown service. Often such a personal directory is really nothing more than a list of someone's "favorite sites" on the Web. Since these kinds of personal home pages are not likely to be listed in the larger, subject-based directories, they are not so easy to find. Often only the Web's search vehicles, as they are called, will enable you to locate them (see the next section). In fact, personal directories typically are created by people who do their own formal searches as well as their own serendipitous surfing.

How Do I Find Stuff That's Not Organized in Directories?

This is the question of questions on the Web. In fact, more and more people are saying that the ones who will really make money on the Internet are those who can sell the means for people to find stuff online. No existing directories are comprehensive; they can't be, since everything is changing every day.

> **"The best way to find information and resources on the Web, after you've exhausted the standard directories, is to use one of the so-called search engines."**

Search engines (what a crazy term) are nothing more than computer programs that "search" the Web for key words. You don't put the program on your computer or search the Web yourself. Instead, you use someone else's program on *their* computer. You "go to" that search computer's address on the Web, just as you would go to any other URL. Once there, you fill out that computer's graphical "forms" to give it search information (what you're looking for). In other words, search engines allow you to communicate with another computer, using *that* Net computer and its software to search the Web. These search engines periodically scan parts of the Web, collecting information for their own computers. When you use the engine, it searches through the material it has collected on the search-engine computer, searching the Web for the key words that you provide. These "searching" computers are set up simply to provide this kind of search service for others, either free or sometimes for a small fee.

I've included a list of some of the more valuable search engines in the appendix. Each of them searches different parts of the Web or searches in a different way. Consequently, you can't get a comprehensive search simply by using one search engine. Moreover, they can be quite busy, which means that either the search-engine computer won't let you connect to it or it will take quite a long time to give you the results of the search.

You'll need to master three or four search engines if you plan to use the Web for significant research (or for serious searches for "fun" stuff). You'll need to master the following:

1. Know what each search engine searches and what it excludes,

2. Know how to conduct the search in the most efficient and effective way, and

3. Know how to make sense of the results of your search.

1. What does the "engine" search?

Normally the home page of the search engine will tell you what it searches, or the home page will give you a hypertext link to a page that explains this information. Beware that some of the most popular search engines search only a directory of the Web, not all of the Web pages themselves. Some engines search only the "titles" of pages on the Web (what it says at the top of the window of the page). Others search more of the text in each page. Some focus the search on commercial or "for-profit" pages, while others specialize in educational and other non-profit pages. Read the information provided at the home page of the search engine before you launch into your search. Know thy search engine!

2. How does one search efficiently and effectively?

The biggest problem with conducting Web searches is getting too many *hits* — positive responses resulting in pages that you have to peruse. The way to avoid this is to plan your search according to appropriate key words.

If you're interested in information about Christians involved in collegiate hockey, for instance, you had better be careful. If you searched the word "sports" you would likely produce hundreds of thousands of hits — if the engine even accepted your search. It might tell you to take a hike, hardly the sport you were thinking about.

"*Booleans* are ways of combining key words in your search in order to make it more effective."

All of the best search engines permit you to use *booleans* — words or symbols used to "connect" numerous key search words. For example, we could combine the words "Christian" and "hockey," asking the engine to give us only pages that use *both* words ("both" and "and" are typical booleans). Certainly this would help us. Other booleans include "or" (to search one or another combination of words, e.g.).

But we could go a step further. Some engines permit the user to include multiple versions of words in the search. If the engine permits it, then, we could do something like "Christian*" and "hockey," where the asterisk indicates that we would accept any ending on the word "Christian," such as "Christianity" and "Christians" as well as "Christian." I particularly like engines that permit you to use combinations of words that appear only in sequence in the original document. In other words, we could ask the engine to search only for "Christian hockey," where the two words are side by side in the original document. It's possible that none of these special kinds of searches would be necessary, but you never know.

Finally, the best searching seeks information about specific people or organizations. You won't be inundated with information that includes the key words but is unrelated to your interests (unless you search for a common name, e.g., *John Smith*, which would yield far too many responses). So if we had the name of a hockey team or a hockey player, we would be far better off than simply searching around under "hockey" or "Christian" or any other key words. When possible, use proper names or places.

3. Using the search results.

Unless you are doing a very specific search using proper nouns, you will find that you get many useless findings. You can waste hours looking through the pages that your search said contained the key words. Here are a few pointers to minimize that problem.

First, try skipping the pages whose title or description seems not to be related to the topic of your search. In the vast majority of cases, it is unrelated.

Second, go first to the pages that are directories. You may suddenly find that someone else has already compiled a directory on the topic of your interest.

Third, if you go to a page that your search located, and you find that it is a long, text-filled page (I've seen 20- "pages"), don't waste a half hour looking for the key words in the document. Instead, using either your web browser's "find" (look under "edit" in the menu) command, search for the key word on the page. If your browser does not have this feature, copy the text from the page, paste it in an open page in your word-processing program, and use that program's "find in page" or equivalent command.

How Do You Find E-Mail Addresses of People?

In some respects, e-mail addresses are even more personal than postal addresses because they deliver mail inside a home, directly to a person's computer.

If it's hard to find Web pages for various topics and organizations, it's far more difficult to locate the e-mail addresses of persons. Some of this is understandable: e-mail addresses are much like postal addresses, and people value their privacy. In some respects, e-mail addresses are even more personal than postal addresses because they deliver mail inside a home, directly to a person's computer.

You will be surprised, though, how many individuals have their own home pages on the Web. The better search engines will find these home pages, and in almost every case the personal home pages include personal e-mail addresses.

There are no comprehensive e-mail directories, any more than there are comprehensive telephone books. By the time these directories go to publication, most of the e-mail addresses would be changed, anyway; extremely well-known people are not going to allow their e-mail addresses to be published in such a book. Most of the addresses in those kinds of books are either no longer usable or are actually business addresses that go to a secretary or business manager's office. Some of the most helpful e-mail directories are listed in the appendix.

The commercial online services give subscribers the option of listing their addresses in online directories. In some cases the people you might wish to reach will have their names and e-mail addresses listed in those directories. In fact, I've been amazed at how many people I've located, and how many people have located me, in this manner. The problem, of course, is that you have to be a subscriber to the online service, such as CompuServe, in order to use its member directory. If you know that someone you are looking for subscribes to one of the services, see if one of your friends subscribes to that service; ask the friend to check the member directory. MCI and a few other Internet access providers also have directories of their users.

Often you can get someone's e-mail address simply by going through the person's institution. Schools and universities, for instance, generally maintain e-mail phone books accessible through the Web. Some corporations and a growing number of denominations do as well. Ministries are beginning to get on this bandwagon, but, ironically, they have been slow to catch on even though they often pride themselves in communication. Use the Web search engines or directories to find the home page of the organization. Then scour the home page for any information about "who we are" or "directories." If you don't find anything, send an e-mail note to the person listed as being in charge of the web site (usually "webmaster@*name of org*"), requesting assistance in locating the person's e-mail address. If the organization is not on the Web, but does have e-mail addresses, send your inquiry to "postmaster" instead of the "webmaster" at the same address (the *postmaster* is the person(s) most responsible for mail traffic at the site).

A quick review of the nature of e-mail addresses might help you through this process. All addresses include three parts. My address at the Gospel Communications Network, for instance, is:

schu@gospelcom.net

The first part, the "schu," is my personal designation (short for my last name, Schultze). After the "@" symbol (which means "at") is the "domain" name, which really means the computer that receives and stores my e-mail at the Gospel Communications Network (the "gospelcom" computer). Finally, after the period (or "dot," as Web people frequently say), there is the designation for the kind of organization or institution; the "net" designation means it is a "network" (don't worry about the specifics of what that means). Here are some of the more typical endings for e-mail addresses:

.com (company)
.edu (educational institution)
.gov (governmental)

Two additional insights might be helpful. First, if you are communicating with someone who is using one of the commercial online services, you can know the last two sections of their address if you know which service they use. Since these services are companies, they end in the usual "com." Moreover, the name of the service is the same as the domain computer, such as "compuserve," "prodigy" and "aol" (for America Online). Second, Internet e-mail addresses originating from other countries end not in the "com" and "edu" endings, but in a particular country code (e.g., "au" for Australia and "uk" for United Kingdom).

I have had quite a bit of success getting peoples' e-mail addresses through the e-mail *lists* (or *listservs,* as they are sometimes called). I cover these lists in more detail in the appendix. Let me just say for now that these kinds of mailing lists are made up of groups of people with common interests (e.g., one list is for people who are interested in the relationship between religion and communication). When you subscribe to one, you get all of the mail that any subscriber sends to the list address. If you "post" a message requesting someone's e-mail address, hundreds and even thousands of people may read it. Assuming that you have posted the inquiry on a list made up of people familiar with the life and/or work of the person whose e-mail address you seek, you will likely get a positive response if that person is active on e-mail. The appendix includes information for subscribing without charge to many lists of interest to Christians. You can do it quickly and automatically with an e-mail message.

Seek and Ye Might Find

Unfortunately, the Net is not organized nearly as well as one would like. And things may get worse before they get better because of enormous growth of the Web, in particular. I see e-mail addresses on more and more business cards, but I also know that some people feel so overwhelmed by the amount of e-mail that they get that they are considering having two, separate addresses — one for junk mail that goes straight to cyber trash, and one to give only to a fairly select group of friends and colleagues. I understand this, but I have mixed feelings about it. Ministries, for example, need to be accountable, and any kind of regular public contact should help make them more accountable to at least the people they most immediately serve.

On the Web, search vehicles and directories are improving so quickly that the major hurdles discussed in this chapter will be largely overcome in the next few years. However, I think that it will be commercial organizations that are most able to afford the resources for such Net organization. This will undoubtedly mean that Net organization will improve at a cost. Meanwhile, personal home pages, and personal home-page directories, will continue to spring up all over the Web. Some of these will be religious directories of considerable value to the Christian community. I'll do my best to keep you posted on these in my e-mail newsletter, *Internet for Christians* (see appendix). I'll also continue to post at my Virtual Appendix some of the best e-mail directories (go to http://www.gospelcom.net/ifc).

CHAPTER FIVE

Ministering Via the Internet

In the preface I suggested that the Internet was part of the unfolding of God's Creation. I also said that Christians have a responsibility to use the Net for the glory of God. This chapter directly addresses that goal. Getting you on the Net and used to the Net's idiosyncrasies is one thing. It's far more important to help you use the Net in ways that will truly minister to other people and bring glory to our Lord and Savior, Jesus Christ.

Let me start, though, with one observation about "doing ministry." I do not use this term narrowly to refer only to full-time ministers or only to people who are paid to minister to others. Nor do I use the term "minister" to refer only to evangelistic activities. Evangelism is certainly a crucial goal for all us, but not all of us are called or gifted to preach the word or lead evangelistic rallies. In other words, not all of us are called to be evangelists on the Net, but we are indeed all a witness for good or for bad to the reality of Jesus Christ. Everything we do on the Net reflects something of what we believe and value— every word that we type, every image that we compose, every link that we "jump" from one site to another.

In my view, our lives are a witness — even the lives we live on, in and through the Internet, the World Wide Web and e-mail. So this chapter is not merely for people who are called to be evangelists or for people who are in full-time ministry. It's written for all believers in Christ who use the Net for business, pleasure, family communication and the like. Of course, most of my examples will be taken from Net sites of direct ministry, since I do indeed hope to help people who will be using the Internet to spread the Word and to further the Kingdom of God in cyberspace. Nevertheless, most of the kinds of ministry I discuss can be undertaken by lay persons as well as ministers.

"Each of us has special gifts and talents that may be very applicable to the Net, including writing, graphics, schmoozing, technical computer networking, site design, teaching, data-base management and all the rest. If we all used such abilities as Christians on the Net, the Christian presence would be a magnificent testimony to the Lordship of Christ!"

In short, you don't have to be a pastor to minister on the Net; in fact, I hope that some of you will minister to pastors! Ministry is not just for the professionals, but for all of us as we are gifted. One of the incredible things about the Net is the extent to which the average, gifted person can create worthwhile resources, directories, discussion groups, mailing lists, periodicals, book reviews, news reports, and the like.

How Can a Lay Person Use the Net?

Let's assume that the vast majority of Christian Internet users are not involved in full-time ministry. How can they make worthwhile use of the Internet?

Lay Christians have two major options. First, they can use the Net for their own spiritual growth. Second, they can contribute to the work of various ministries, some of whom might need considerable help creating and implementing strategies for Internet ministry.

So far the development on the Net of lay-oriented resources for personal ministry has been rather limited. Clearly the potential is significant. At the invitation of Nick Hengeveld, who was then webmaster for the Gospel Communications Network, Radio Bible Class put its daily devotional, *Our Daily Bread,* on the World Wide Web at http://www.gospelcom.net/rbc/.

"Using an interactive, graphic-calendar format, the *Our Daily* Bread devotional has been accessed by many thousands of people literally all over the world. With no publicity or fanfare, the Internet's version of the devotional was discovered and used by an amazing array of people, some of whom do not have access to paper copies of any devotionals."

The Bible Gateway, which provides multiple English translations and a growing number of other language translations in digital form on the Web, has been similarly popular throughout the world. Clearly the easy accessibility of translations, accessed by Bible chapter, scripture passage and the like, is sought by many lay Christians for their own study and devotions. When Nick put the Spanish version of the scriptures on the Gateway, he received a response from a Mexican Christian within minutes, correcting some of the Spanish! There had not been any publicity or promotion telling people that the Spanish-language scriptures would be online soon, although he had received requests for them.

In recent years a number of leading evangelical theologians have decried the low biblical and especially theological literacy of American Christians. The Internet may be able to help with this problem, particularly through distance-learning from seminaries, divinity schools and Christian colleges. Unfortunately, this area has been slow to develop, partly because seminaries themselves have not been at the forefront of media technology; seminaries generally have been among the slowest to adopt new media, and most pastors themselves are ill-equipped to use audio and video, let alone computers and the Internet. But for lay Christians who are willing to spend some time searching the Web, there is a vast array of theological information, papers, book summaries and the like available free of charge (see appendix). This should grow considerably as journals and newsletters move to online publishing to cut costs and boost readership.

Lay Christians can also benefit from the many e-mail lists (sometimes called *listservs* or *majordomos*) dealing with Christian issues and topics. Some of these lists may be populated extensively by academicians and pastors, but educated lay participants typically are warmly welcomed. The nice thing about such lists is that one does not have to participate; you can simply "read the mail," learning what you have time for and jumping into the discussion only as you feel you have the time, energy or expertise. These lists do not usually charge subscriptions. The appendix includes a fairly extensive list of Christian-related lists, but among those potentially of interest to lay people are "CHRISTIA," a discussion of living the practical Christian life, "BIBLES," a Bible-study-oriented list, and "SCICHR-L," a discussion of science and Christianity.

Lay Christians can also use the Net to order Bible-study resources. There are sites that sell books, Bibles, videos, Christian computer software, Bible reference materials, church education resources, and just about everything else you could think of.

Christian periodicals have been slow to go online, but it looks like that will be changing soon. Christianity Today, Inc., launched its array of periodicals on America Online, and later added some of them to the World Wide Web. Keep checking my *Internet for Christians* Web listing at http://www.gospelcom.net/ifc for the latest information about online periodicals. There are dozens of Christian periodicals on the Web.

There's a whole array of Web sites out there that I would hardly try to describe in one paragraph, except to call it "miscellaneous." These are sites for Christian singles, denominational information, apologetics, Christian traditions (such as Reformed, Mennonite, Episcopal, Methodist, Roman Catholic), Christian music, international broadcast evangelism, international missions, liturgy, and on and on. As best I can tell, most of these sites' pages are constructed by lay Christians, sometimes for a fee and sometimes as a volunteer effort. Together they represent an enormous investment of time and energy.

It's up to lay Christians as well as ministers to figure out what kinds of Web sites, mailing lists and the like would truly serve people. Much of the email I receive from Christians suggests they are looking online for life-style-related material, such as entertainment reviews and child-rearing help. It seems that Christians are very interested in help with living the Christian life in contemporary society.

What's the Value of the Net for Parish Pastors?

Pastors will have to be increasingly computer literate. Two particularly important aspects of the Net are relevant to its use by the clergy:

1. The development of the Net within the academic community, including many Christian scholars and theologians, and

2. The ease with which the Internet can put pastors in touch with one another.

Although seminaries have been slow to get on the Net, Christian scholars and religious studies folks have made quite a bit of progress. A quick look at the list of Net lists in the appendix shows that there is much significant discussion of religion generally and Christianity, specifically, on these lists. There are lists on the history of and current events within particular Christian traditions and denominations, on cell-based churches, on Catholic spirituality, on Judaic studies, on Greek studies, on apologetics, on preaching the Revised Common Lectionary, and on and on. Again, people are encouraged to use these lists, free of charge. Some of them are lively, important discussion areas for pastors to ask questions as well as to provide responses. Some of them provide book reviews, announcements of conventions and conferences and other helpful information. Try a list for a while; if you don't like it, drop your subscription (see appendix). If you do like it, tell your friends about it, encouraging them to subscribe, too.

Beyond such educational purposes, however, mailing lists can really help pastors stay in touch with one another. Rural pastors, or pastors who lead the only congregation of their tradition in town, can use the Net to develop orbits of friends and associates virtually free of cost. They can exchange sermon ideas, discuss pastoral problems and opportunities, swap personal reactions to periodical essays, books and news, discuss the cultural currents that affect parish life, commiserate about difficulties, pray for one another and, of course, build each other up in the Lord.

Some seminaries are going on the Internet with everything from course schedules and degree information to distance-education for both continuing education and degree programs. I can't imagine that this will replace actual on-campus learning for most students; instead, the Net is opening educational opportunities for people who would not be able to take all of the time necessary to travel to distant campuses. We'll see various kinds of programs combining on-campus and distance-education programs. Some of these will likely not be very good programs, but the more creative schools, which are both computer literate and educationally savvy, will make good use of the new digital technologies.

"The Web, in particular, offers some excellent opportunities for pastors to follow what's happening in contemporary culture."

Web-based research can help pastors with preaching, counseling and other activities that require significant cultural literacy. Because of its close alliance with the entertainment industry, the Web is loaded with sites about current cultural phenomena. Where else can a pastor read the publicity blurbs and see a trailer for a new film without leaving the parsonage? Even more importantly, pastors who are preaching on particular topics can search those subjects across the Web, zeroing in on precisely the quotes, data, or perspectives they need. They can fill their Web browser's *hot spots* or *bookmarks* (favorite addresses of the places they visit regularly on the Web) with the most valuable periodicals, creating a virtual library of their own at minimal cost.

If all of this is not enough evidence of the potential value of the Internet to pastors, consider as well the developing use of the Internet by book publishers, including religious book publishers. One of the advantages of the Web for book publicity is the minimal cost involved in publishing sample chapters online. This will undoubtedly help pastors and others to peruse more carefully the actual offerings of publishers, not just the glitzy catalog blurbs and commendations. In addition, we can expect that the more visionary religious publishers will personalize their Web sites, providing e-mail addresses for some authors and certainly giving Web users an opportunity now and then to chat online with Christian authors.

Finally, I should mention the growing affinity between Web publishing and the CD-ROM industry. CD-ROMs are like the CDs that store recorded music ("ROM" means "read-only memory," which simply indicates that the consumers cannot re-record on the CD; they can only "play" them). It is commonly assumed in Internet circles that the formats used for publishing on the Web and the formats used in reference-based CD-ROM products will be merged. In other words, we should expect a continued growth in Bible and theological reference materials on both the Web and CD-ROM (or whatever digital formats will replace the CD-ROM). As pastors are trained to use traditional reference materials in a new form on their personal computers, they will simultaneously be learning how to use such materials on the Internet. One likely scenario suggests that book publishers will sell digital versions of their products online, and that pastors and other users will be able to download those products right to their computers in the parsonage.

> **"In my judgment, the search capabilities alone (e.g., the ability to search in seconds all volumes of John Calvin's *Institutes* for a key word or phrase — how about "fun?") — will increasingly lead seminaries and their graduates to 'think digitally.'"**

How Can Youth Workers Use the Net?

Hang on to your cyberhats on this one. I can't imagine youth leaders in today's world who are not at least *computer* savvy, if not Net savvy. Why? Because kids are learning computers like some people learn second languages — younger and younger. The "cybergap" between adults and children is going to get worse before it gets better. Kids will be living literally in different cultures than their parents inhabit. Youth workers have an opportunity to speak the same computer language and the same Internet dialect that their youth speak. Just like youth leaders have to know something about young peoples' music, or something about MTV, they'll have to know about the Net culture. If they don't, they run the risk of being perceived as irrelevant dinosaurs.

> **"Net-surfing is increasingly important for youth workers — as important as watching teen flicks and catching an occasional rock concert."**

The music industry, for example, has been saying in the trade journals that the Internet represents the first significant promotional vehicle since MTV — and perhaps even a better promotional vehicle. The movie industry has already taken the Web by storm, generating sites to launch new movies with visual and aural appeal. These are high-quality, multi-media Web pages, not the drab, text-oriented stuff at most of the universities. Even the Christian music industry has launched well-conceived Web sites for artists such as Charlie Peacock (see the "music" section in crosssearch at http://www.crosssearch.com). The appeal to teens is not just computers, but endless multi-media entertainment, the ultimate Web surf that never ends as more and more material is put online every day.

What's a youth leader to do in this multi-media extravaganza?

Choice one: Stick your head in the old media and hope that computers go away.

Choice two: Persuade your congregation's parents and pastors to keep kids from getting online.

Choice three — the only realistic one — Get online with the kids and on your own to see, hear and read what's going on. Only this option can produce enough discernment and wisdom about the digital revolution to give youth leaders some anchors in the forceful stream of technology. Only the last option will help youth workers relate to growing numbers of computer-savvy, Net-hoppin' kids with jazzed-up modems, rip-roaring keyboards and big-screen monitors.

Let's consider some of the opportunities for youth workers on the Net. First, mailing lists are made to order for ongoing discussion of the ups and downs of working with today's youth. It seems to me that lists of youth workers, sharing their ideas and passing along tips, is nearly invaluable. Because of the turnover in youth ministry, leaders tend to have to reinvent the ministry over and over again. This is not bad, since youth culture changes and each youth leader has to find his or her own style. But without some youth-worker forums the job will be much tougher for most leaders. The beauty of mailing lists is the way they can fit into a youth leader's existing schedule; he or she can check the messages and respond daily, once a week, or whatever works — even at midnight, after the teens have gone home — we hope! Moreover, mailing lists can easily be *archived* (stored for others to read) on the Web, even by topic of discussion, so that future leaders can learn from previous discussion.

Second, the Web can greatly improve youth leaders' access to ministry resources. By and large, youth leaders have not had particularly well-organized, timely means of reviewing and adopting ministry resources. They may not receive youth-ministry resource catalogs when they need them; in fact, they might not even get many of the mailings, especially if the church's previous youth ministry didn't use the catalogs and the church doesn't receive them. Moreover, the leaders might be uncertain about the content of particular videos, curricular materials and the like. On the Web, youth-ministry resources can be put into "virtual" centers that are updated as new resources are available. More than that, the centers can include samples of all of the materials, including audio, video, text, graphics and the like. If all of this were not enough, the more Web-savvy youth-ministry resource providers will include information about how the materials have been used successfully by youth leaders — perhaps even with e-mail addresses for those leaders!

"The Web could provide a terrific way for youth leaders to stay on top of contemporary youth culture — a daunting task for any adult!"

Because the Web is loaded with material on music groups, movies, television and the like, it is entirely possible for anyone to create online "directories" to the pages that include information about these kinds of youth culture. Youth Specialties (http://www.gospelcom.net/ys/) has already launched one of these directories. The beauty of creating this type of resource is that it remains "virtual" because it can be continually updated. For example, if the original directory includes a link to the site of a particular rock group, the link benefits from any changes made to the original site, as long as the rock group's original address (*URL*) remains the same.

Finally, parachurch youth ministries can benefit through faster, less-expensive communication among their staff. Through the use of mailing lists, personal e-mail, resource centers, and the like, organizations like Youth for Christ (http://www.gospelcom.net/yfc/) can create effective new webs of communication among their workers (see appendix). It seems to me that the Net should improve the viability of such parachurch groups in rapidly changing culture. Local youth workers can have far more input into national decision-making; the national organization, in turn, can do a far better job of serving the day-to-day needs of their staff. But all of this is possible, of course, only if the national offices have the vision and resources to establish a significant Net presence as well as to encourage and equip their staffs get into the new media.

What's on the Net for Missionaries?

Missionaries' use of the Internet reflects both the tremendous opportunity and the considerable frustrations involved in going high-tech. The benefits of missionaries' access to the Net, in particular, is fairly obvious. But guaranteeing reliable, secure international access even to simple e-mail can be a major hassle. Moreover, computers and Net use can be expensive in an international context. These problems will have to worked out, however, because of the needs of business persons and educators in the same countries and cities. Missionaries should be able to take advantage of the technological improvements being made around the world for other purposes, in countries as diverse as China and India.

But how will local, native populations view high-tech missionary work by outsiders? Obviously, this depends heavily on the culture, but it certainly could be a reason not use Net communication. Computers are increasingly international and cross-cultural, but they are not value-free in the eyes of a given culture. Often only the upper classes of a society have computers. What kind of witness would it be for rural missionaries to launch into computer communication in the midst of this type of cultural context? These are difficult issues, indeed, but the benefits of computers should still be considered in appropriate settings and at appropriate times.

Missionaries are heavily involved in two types of communication. First is the day-to-day communication in the field. In developing areas, this communication will not be significantly improved by the Internet because of a lack of dependable local networks, computer facilities and the like. Second, missionaries are often extensively involved in communication outside of the local orbit of missionary work. The latter includes communication with home churches, family and friends, sponsors, denominational and parachurch missions offices, missionaries in other areas and the like. All of this type of communication could be enhanced considerably by e-mail, which can be far more timely and more reliable than *snail mail* (postal mail), and in many cases considerably less expensive than voice telephone calls.

Some of the benefits are obvious: faster and more frequent prayer requests from the field, more regular and meaningful communication with loved ones back home, prompt requests for funding in cases of emergency, and so forth. But less obvious are the benefits to the *quality* of ministry. Missionaries, like youth ministers, often seem to be reinventing the cultural wheel — simultaneously studying the culture and language while trying to minister to people. Perhaps the ease of regular communication with other missionaries in similar cultures, or even with missionaries who served previously in the same culture or field, would enhance the work of missionaries. Moreover, the Web is home to all kinds of anthropological publications, research reports, discussions and the like; missionaries can "listen in" on these discussions and read these findings. The Web also has all kinds of information about current political situations in many unstable regions of the world. A growing number of governments publish their official statements about personal safety and political and social unrest. These kinds of material are rapidly being indexed in country- and region-specific directories, which missionaries can use.

> **"E-mail can function as a kind of interactive journal among a small group of cultural insiders, continuously refining cultural understanding and fine-tuning missionaries' approaches to ministry."**

In the cases of language learning and Bible translation, the Net could provide the daily or weekly forum for informal education among a group of missionaries facing the same struggles. Private mailing lists and message-posting boards offer a kind of "virtual dialogue" of hermeneutical and theological issues. Simple e-mail facilitates regular, daily, even hourly communication between several missionaries or even among a group of missionaries with similar interests and needs.

Finally, I would like to address the overall issue of ongoing missionary education. Perhaps the Net could more effectively integrate such education with the day-to-day work of missionaries by enabling some education during the fieldwork, not just during the furloughs back home. For example, my colleague at Calvin College, Dr. Robert Fortner, Director of Graduate Studies, reports that there is considerable interest among some missions groups in studying through Internet-based field education. In communication studies, there are many nationals and internationals who never received extensive formal education in the discipline. Working with the International Communications Research for Evangelism Consortium, he has offered a variety of workshops on audience research. These and many other courses could be offered at least partly via the Net.

For all of these potential benefits, however, the technical problems can be enormously frustrating for missionaries who venture into the field in hopes of maintaining computer-based communication. Not only does the computer equipment have to be maintained, but so do the telephone lines and networks that provide the digital conduits to the outside world. Then there are the software problems associated with Internet providers and the commercial online services. Some ministries have reduced these problems considerably simply by using long-distance phone calls back to a denominational or parachurch computer system to post and receive messages. While this works, it hardly creates the kind of inexpensive communication system that would really encourage its use. The declining costs of laptop computers and the growing worldwide Internet infrastructure will undoubtedly improve the situation in many developing countries.

Should Congregations Take to the Net?

I pose this as a serious question, not a rhetorical one. Lately all kinds of local churches have started putting home pages on the Web. As I peruse these pages, however, I often can't figure out exactly what the purpose is of publishing them on an international network. Are the parishes trying to attract people who will be moving into the area? Perhaps. More often it seems to me that someone simply got the idea that the church should have a presence on the Web. So they created a home page. Beyond that, there's not much purpose.

> ## "I don't think local churches should get involved institutionally with the Internet unless the Net enhances their ministry."

I have no doubt that God can use something like a congregational Web page to bring potential new members through the doors on Sunday, but surely this method is not as efficient or as effective a use of resources than many other techniques. Nor do I think that a church can significantly change its local image by publishing on the Web (e.g., creating the image of a friendly, helping congregation). And I'm not even so enthusiastic about using the Web as a kind of bulletin board for local congregations to promote special events. All of these techniques may work to some degree, but are they really the best uses at this stage in the Internet's development?

I don't think so. Instead, I would suggest that for the time being congregations consider the use of simple e-mail and mailing lists *if* a significant percentage of the congregation or church leaders is online. I say this for the following reasons:

1. E-mail is far more personal and interactive, which is what a local congregation should be,

2. E-mail is easily adapted to existing communication needs within a congregation, and

3. E-mail is extremely easy to set up and administer.

Here are some possible uses of e-mail by local churches:

- Electronic prayer chains that automatically send requests to all subscribers

- Church news lists for congregational "alumni" who have moved away but still support the congregation and appreciate news (this could be especially important for smaller, home-missions churches that need the support)

- E-mail lists for church administrators, elders, deacons and the like, informing them of meetings, special concerns, business agendas, etc.

- Reminder lists that inform members of their irregular duties at upcoming services

- Sermon-discussion lists

- Special kids' lists that simply encourage them to exchange messages with their friends in the congregation

- Congregation-wide lists for weekly mailings about upcoming sermon topics, summer worship hours, special-service times, committee meetings and the like

None of these uses of e-mail is particularly exciting, especially contrasted with a full-color graphic "Welcome!" on the Web. But for the time being, they are far more realistic and useful approaches to the Net. No doubt as the Web grows there will be increasing "competition" among local congregations to have the best-looking Web pages in town. If anything, I think that youth ministry might be a better reason to begin Web sites. After all, youth are generally more Internet-savvy than adults, and they like the multi-media impact. Perhaps some churches could commission their youth groups to create Web sites for the congregation. In this context, the work would not merely give a Web presence to the congregation, but more importantly would give youth a chance to use their skills and creativity for the good of the congregation.

What's a Denomination to Do with the Internet?

I fear that this entire topic could easily become very divisive. As I scan the Net and the various commercial online services, I see much de- nominational use of computer-to-computer communication that is sim- ply not very worthwhile. Perhaps denominational prelates feel some pressure to move into cyberspace — one more area to develop *before* the parachurch groups take charge. Perhaps some denominational offices believe — or at least hope — that computers can provide the denomina- tional glue to keep together churches that are being divided by the culture wars. Maybe there is even some implicit or explicit theological sense that the new media simply have to be claimed for Christ, and that one denomination may be more gifted or experienced to make this happen.

I don't know all of the motivations for denominational forays into cyberspace, but I do know that there is a tremendous amount of confusion. The Internet and the commercial online services generally are not being used very effectively. The most important questions denominations can ask themselves about the new medium is how it can enhance existing activities and current forms of communication without eliciting reactions that reduce denominational loyalty and encourage primarily denominational criticism.

> **"If denominations launch into cyberspace without looking at the bigger picture, they may find themselves in the middle of a cyber-boomerang."**

Overall, online communication seems to have eroded denominational ties as much as it has strengthened them. The simple reason is that e-mail, in particular, tends to be counter-institutional; it turns communication patterns upside down and gives more relative status and visibility to dissident groups and individuals. On e-mail the denominational prelates and average souls in the pew have equal footing — unless a denomination tries to create top-down traffic patterns, which are not likely to work very well. Online services and the Internet generally make it easier for dissidents and disenfranchised members to organize and to act collectively. These folks can't afford to publish their own magazine, but they can certainly foot the online bill to bombard prelates with questions, pepper them with concerns and even blast them for real or alleged misdeeds. It's not surprising, then, that some of the "reform" movements within denominations have established alternative news services via computer networks.

In no way do I wish to suggest that this kind of high-tech culture war within denominations is entirely bad, but I do think that it's part of the bigger picture that denominations have to consider. Denominations, like all institutions, must change or they may find that they are serving the hierarchy more than the people in the trenches of life. Computer-to-computer communication can put additional pressure on denominations to be sensitive to the feelings, beliefs, and needs of average church-goers, especially if the denominational leaders organize the communication to help them be more sensitive. This kind of "feedback," in my judgment, is potentially a very valuable service to the denomination. It's particularly better than letters-to-the-editor columns and other feedback mechanisms that greatly limit the voices heard and tend to be easily discounted as unrepresentative.

What can denominational leaders do to encourage such feedback? At a minimum, denominational publications should include editors' e-mail addresses to encourage fairly effortless responses from readers. Denominational e-mail discussion forums (mailing lists open to all denominational members) is one further step in the right direction. This must be monitored, however, to nip in the bud outlandish rumors or particularly unkind messages which, if not responded to quickly, could generate rumors and innuendo through the off-line gossip channels as well as through the cyber networks. Finally, denominational documents, such as reports of study committees and official proposals for denominational change, should include e-mail addresses for "public" denominational responses.

Beyond the limitations of e-mail are Web-related opportunities that few denominations have taken advantage of so far. Because of the relatively low cost of Net publishing, denominations would be wise to consider including copies of their official, public communication in on-going Web files. Everything from the agendas and minutes of denominational committee meetings to official annual pronouncements, church polity and catalogs for instructional materials could be published easily on the Web. The Lutheran Church—Missouri Synod has done much to encourage this kind of electronic publishing at least within its own networks. The Southern Baptist Convention on CompuServe has created a relatively unique service that provides current updates to church-education materials, so the examples and illustrations are timely. If nothing else interests denominations about the new technology, leaders should consider the stewardship issues attendant to the monetary and environmental cost of paper publishing.

"Denominations tend to produce an awful lot of paper for bureaucratic communication. Online publishing of

denominational policies and polity is as much a stewardship as a political issue."

Let me suggest, however, that perhaps the most fruitful direction for denominations to take with the Web is educational. Most denominations have their own seminaries, for instance, that should be on the Web, promoting courses, providing helpful information for pastors and other church leaders, explaining church polity, clarifying denominational positions on various issues, and so forth. The gap between seminaries and the pastors, let alone between seminaries and the laity, is often far too wide in many denominations.

Could not seminaries also offer via the Internet credit and non-credit distance education courses for the laity, and for pastors who are unable to get time off from their positions to attend seminary? These might have a shorter on-campus "residency" requirement but include more reading and weekly paper assignments, for example. I can hear the complaints from the theological gurus at the big-name schools: "Further erosion of standards and watering down of real theological education!!" My reply is, "It all depends on how it's done." Standards are set by the faculty and should be upheld by denominational leaders. Distance education can be just as rigorous as on-campus education. Moreover, distance education can be organized creatively to include telephone discussion groups, regional discussion meetings, online discussion and other techniques to create co-learning. Just because a student sits in the classroom does not mean that real learning is taking place. In fact, it has become increasingly clear that seminary degrees are granted in some situations merely as rewards for residency!

Denominational education raises the issue of denominational library resources as well. Up until the last few years the Net has been primarily a vehicle for research, including access to libraries. Seminaries have not been among the leaders in getting library materials online, including card catalogs, theological and pastoral journals and reference materials. In fact, many denominational publications are not even adequately indexed for historical or other research. Denominations could serve not just their own constituency, but all Christians, if they were to pursue an aggressive policy of online publication. Since most publications are now created on computers anyway, they exist in a digital form that could be transferred to the Web or even published online as a text-only filing system. All of this is to suggest that denominations don't have to see themselves so much as geography-based institutions. Computer networks provide an opportunity for these organizations to extend their solidarity and ministry beyond geography and ethnicity.

What's the Future for Parachurch Ministries on the Net?

Not surprisingly, parachurch ministries have been among the leaders in getting on the new computer networks. For one thing, they often have the freedom to adopt new media without all of the denominational bureaucracy. For another, they frequently are looking for new ministry opportunities to expand their mission and to build their constituencies. For yet another, parachurch ministries are generally more attuned to the Great Commission than are denominational groups. Especially in North America, parachurch groups have built many of their movements and programs on the desire to bring the Gospel to the unsaved. In addition, parachurch organizations have tended to look beyond the constraints of geography, whereas denominations have often been anchored in particular ethnic groups located in specific geographical areas.

"This evangelistic thrust undoubtedly leads parachurch groups to new communications media, including the Internet."

On the down side, however, parachurch organizations typically are strapped for cash to put into new media outreach. The lamentable result is that either they don't seriously consider new media or they plow ahead without the necessary resources to do the job well. One sees this already on the Web, where some of the sites are comprised of poorly conceived and inadequately executed pages. Please don't misunderstand me; I'm grateful for all excursions by believers into new media. But the Net is a new medium with its own internal logic and institutional demands. A love for the Lord is certainly a prerequisite for Christian entre into cyberspace, but skill and ability are very important as well. Such skills won't be adequately developed without the necessary training and technology, both of which are considerable costs. Parachurch ministries will have to develop new, probably younger supporting publics to meet the needs ahead in the new digital media. If they don't, their forays into the new technology could produce low-quality endeavors that are themselves poor witnesses to the Lordship of Christ.

Here, as I see them, are some of the major opportunities for parachurch groups:

- Effective and inexpensive *communication among staff* at all geographic locations (i.e., internal e-mail systems across offices and locations)

- Direct and immediate *communication with constituency* via e-mail and Web publication

- *Expansion of constituency* through an online presence (even well-established ministries will suddenly hear from people who never knew the ministry existed)

- More effective *communication with volunteers and part-time staff,* who otherwise might feel taken for granted (in fact, some ministries might find online volunteer staff who can create the "pages" on their Web sites)

- A much *broader audience for the ministry's resources* (e.g., for an online catalog or other resource directory)

- *Wider promotion of conventions,* conferences and other meetings (including the possibility of online registration)

- Far more effective *post-convention follow-up* through online interaction (e.g., online discussion of convention sessions, including ongoing e-mail with convention speakers and other participants, session evaluations, suggestions for the next convention, availability of tapes of sessions, sources for further reading on convention topics, prayer chains to encourage local participation in conventions, and so on)

- *Broader promotion of existing ministries* (e.g., putting broadcast program times and stations on the Web, or putting sections of existing paper magazines on the Web)

- *Reduced costs* of sending out paper literature by referring inquiries to the Web or other online versions

- *Selling text-based materials online,* with users *downloading* the material directly to their computers and printing the materials on their own home printers (computer users make online "copies" of pamphlets and even short books)

- Constituency *communication with ministry leaders* (e.g., through special e-mail addresses or even "live" chat times)

- *Product sampling* (e.g., book excerpts, video and audio segments)

These kinds of e-mail and Web activities suggest the range of possibilities for parachurch ministries using the new digital technologies and computer-to-computer communication. In chapter seven I will cover some of the basics of Web publishing, since this will undoubtedly be the major online growth area for many ministries in the next few years. Suffice it to say here that the more innovative parachurch groups have to look closely at their goals.

> **"The Net may not fit the existing missions statement of some parachurch groups, and then the organization will have to make the hard decisions about whether or not to change its purpose, or at least broaden it, to fit the new technologies."**

In addition, parachurch organizations have to look seriously at the talents of their staff and volunteers. The Net requires new abilities for maximum benefit. If resources cannot be shifted from one medium to another, additional resources will be required. In the end, this is an opportunity to be pursued wisely and judiciously, not naively. The Net, like all media, is no better or worse than what the people do with it.

Internet Ministry Reconsidered

I like to compare the current state of the Internet with the early days of radio. Back in the 1920s there were all kinds of Christian groups grabbing microphones and transmitters and blasting their "wireless" signals across the ether. Within a decade, most of them had vanished, either through the changing federal rules governing radio station ownership, or more likely through the hapless manner in which many of the stations were created and launched. Enthusiasm is a necessary but rarely sufficient basis for ministry. God grants such enthusiasm, but He also gives the talents and gifts necessary to make the ministry effective. This includes not only the day-to-day workers among the ministry vines, but also the people who support such workers.

As I look over the cyberspace environment, I see an unusual opportunity to invest human resources in this kind of person-to-person approach. Unlike broadcast media, there is something distinctly personal about the Internet. E-mail and the Web are used by individuals, often to communicate directly with other individuals. This kind of grass-roots phenomena will never include everyone because of costs as well as political and technological barriers. Just the other day I read an article about how the Chinese government will attempt to control Internet traffic in the country. And so it goes — for every opportunity there are contrary movements to restrict and prevent communication, to persecute and disparage communicators. Nevertheless, Christians must continue to minister, in the broadest possible sense, to each other and to the rest of the needy world — even through the new world of cyberspace.

CHAPTER SIX

Using the Internet at Home

Once upon a time there were no computers at home. Ten years later, about one-third of all homes in the United States and Canada had home computers. The kids wanted computers for "schoolwork" (and for games, of course). Dad wanted one, too, for work (and for games, of course). Pretty soon families were observed shopping for computers, like they formerly shopped for TV sets or dishwashers.

Once upon a time schools didn't have computers. Not long afterward, schools of all levels, in North America and increasingly the world, had computers. Some affluent school districts even put them in every classroom and hooked up all of the teachers with personal e-mail. Then the school libraries bought computers for CD-ROM reference works. Eventually the schools began teaching courses in computers.

Students from these schools went home and told their parents about computers. Before long these homes had computers, too. Large, discount computer stores opened, selling boxes of computers and related equipment like the supermarkets sell detergent. Company names, like Microsoft, IBM and Apple, became household words.

"Everything was fine until one day the family hooked up their new computer to something called a 'modem.'"

Along with the modem came free software to sign up for an "online information service" — with no charge for a full month! The family hooked up the computer and modem, put the online software in the disk drive, clicked on a fancy icon, and surfed into the cyber-sunset. Life was never the same again.

Does My Family Need to Get on the Net?

It all began so innocently. The family never realized what an "on-line service" really was. The brochure said something about "news, entertainment and information, including your favorite magazines, games and educational services." It all sounded so good.

And so it goes, over and over again in millions of households now joining the cyber revolution. Today it's hard to buy a multi-media computer that doesn't come with a built-in modem and free software to get online. The industry calls it "bundling" — packaging together technology and software that you might not buy separately. So you get to go online whether you'd like to or not.

Let me say right at the start that your family does not have to get on the Internet or any of the commercial online services. This decision is up to the discretion of the parents. Like using a television set or going to movies, the Internet is a choice, not a necessity.

But the fact is that the Internet, even more than the commercial online services, is part of an ongoing digital revolution, not merely a fad. Computer-to-computer communication is the next major wave of media technologies. The technological waves began with simple human speech, continued with writing and eventually printing, and exploded with electronic media, from the telegraph and telephone to broadcasting and satellites. Even if we make concerted efforts as Christian communities to keep these technologies out of our churches, schools, homes and offices, the new media will grow in our midst. They are here to stay.

"In my view, it is unrealistic to keep the new media at bay. Even if we don't buy a computer for our homes, our children will learn how to use them in school and at friends' homes."

The dilemma is similar to the one we face with television. Just as some parents don't permit the one-eyed monster in their homes, perhaps even more will refuse to get a computer, or at least a modem. Some parents will decide to delay inviting computers into their homes at least until the children have formed good study habits and learned to communicate well in writing, listening and speaking. To be honest, this is a perfectly reasonable route to go, and we did something similar by limiting the amount of time our children could spend with television and computers.

There is a spiritual drawback, however, to having a computer-free home. The more monastic approach to the new media ignores a major parental responsibility to teach children about the real world. In short, Christian parents are responsible for teaching discernment, which cannot be developed adequately without real interaction with the world outside of the home. Moreover, parents have responsibility, along with educators, pastors and the like, to develop discernment about *culture*, the creations of human beings. As I suggest in my book and video series, *Winning Your Kids Back from the Media*, communications media are cultural conduits for values, beliefs and actions. They teach us how to think, what to believe and how to act. One of my colleagues at Calvin College, Bill Romanowski, a former youth worker, likes to say that the media play a crucial instructional role in the lives of North American youth. Adolescents learn about life from the media. Now along comes the Internet.

In most homes, then, the question is really *how* to integrate computers and especially computer-to-computer communication into family life. Once the computer is hooked up to a modem, it imports the outside world directly into the home, often in a very personal way through e-mail.

"Modems transform computers into significant cultural transmitters and receivers requiring adequate discernment."

Computer discernment requires at least a sense of *balance* and *appropriateness*. Parents need to strive for balance among the various media, making sure that their offspring are developing their abilities as writers and speakers, and not just computer geeks or hackers. Moreover, parents have to teach appropriate use of the digital media. This includes teaching morality, civility (much needed on the Net), justice (speaking up for those in need, including those who don't have computers or even access to the Net) and love (putting other people ahead of themselves, in contrast to the selfish ways that so many people approach the Internet).

Finally, parents need to encourage their youth to develop their God-given abilities as computer communicators. All of this is stewardship of the medium, and all of it needs to be taught by parents as well as by educators, pastors and other leaders.

Where Should You Put the Computer in the House?

The growing popularity of the Internet and the commercial on-line services suggests that computers are no longer just personal technologies. Instead, computers are becoming *social* technologies, fostering various kinds of interaction among people. The modem connects the computer to the outside world, transforming the computer into a communications medium. As a medium, the computer is a window on the outside world. Its location deserves just as much consideration as decisions about where to put the television set or stereo system. In fact, the highly private use of computers, even more than television, suggests the need for greater caution. Televisions gather people together around the video hearth, whereas computers typically promote private, individualistic communication with the outside world.

For this reason, it makes an awful lot of sense to locate the computer in a fairly public part of the home, and not in a child's bedroom or even in a remote corner of a family room or living room. Children need to be taught from the beginning that the use of the computer for communication has consequences for all members of the family, not just for themselves. They also need to know that computer communication is just as significant as other, more public forms of communication, such as television.

> **"Recurring cases of child-luring via the Internet and commercial online services have shown how susceptible children are to computer-to-computer communication."**

When a child initiates discussion even with strangers via the computer, the communication seems *personal* and *safe* — personal because of the one-to-one nature of the message flow, and safe because the communication occurs within the normally safe boundaries of the home. Children who are shy or emotionally disturbed are particularly susceptible to this kind of computer-induced pseudo-relationship. We know from numerous studies of computer-to-computer communication that anonymity (no prior relationship among communicators) creates the seedbed for artificially intimate relationships (like talking openly with a stranger on a plane). Child-luring by pedophiles and other disturbed people is merely one kind of evidence for these computer-based pseudo-relationships.

Parental safeguards are necessary as the webs of online communication continue to expand and the entry to such webs gets easier. Unless parents locate the computer in a place where modem communication can be monitored, there is a fairly good likelihood that *any* child will develop some unhealthy online relationships. Even if you don't subscribe to an Internet access provider or a commercial online service, there is always the possibility of either a local, BBS-based (computer bulletin board system) relationship or direct, computer-to-computer relationships.

In many communities there is BBS (computer bulletin board service) availability without cost. These are like mini-networks that use one main computer in a community. Local residents call a number to connect their computer to the BBS computer, thereby also connecting to others who connect to the main computer. Users of these services typically form local clubs and begin interacting socially at business meetings and club activities. Once friendships are made via these BBS groups, it is possible for members to exchange messages directly between their personal computers, without going through the BBS computer. This type of communication can be extremely private. Therefore, the need for parental monitoring is great, indeed, and some of the newer "lockout" software that prohibits people from entering particular online arenas can be an additional safeguard.

Locating the computer in a fairly public spot in the house also has the advantage of transforming the personal computer into a family event. There is a growing amount of group-oriented computer software, including games, that families could enjoy together. Even making simple graphics, such as drawing cartoons or creating family stationery, can be a family project. Our kids have always enjoyed creating on computer their own greeting cards and special messages for friends and family. While some of this might require privacy, it is off-line work, not communication with the outside world via computer. If the computer is located in a family-oriented part of the house, it will foster collective use, family interaction and even mutual instruction about how to use the crazy thing! Believe me, adults can learn a lot from computer-savvy kids.

The only major drawback to locating the family computer in a high-traffic area in the home is the difficulty of concentrating on some computer work. After all, many families use computers for schoolwork and business-related work as well as for leisure. There are times when children and parents alike will want to focus quietly on the computer, without noisy interference and without a parade of snoopy family members. We've found, however, that there are always times of day when this is not a problem, such as early mornings during summers and weekends, mid-evening (when most people are out or relaxing with a book or newspaper), and even late evening (especially for the parents).

What are the Educational Benefits of the Internet for the Family?

The Net was started for educational and research purposes, and it continues to be an incredible resource for people who want to learn about almost anything. While the Internet is certainly loaded with fun sites, especially on the Web, it is still primarily an educational resource. In my judgment, supervised use of the Net can contribute significantly to a child's education. Moreover, the Net can encourage adults to continue their own, informal education.

Perhaps the most impressive educational use of the Net is school-related research. Most children have relatively limited access to materials in their own school libraries, such as reference and trade books, maybe a few CD-ROM encyclopedias, and, in some cases, periodical databases also on CD-ROM. Obviously children need to master these kinds of resources in their school libraries. But the Net opens up a child's research potential far beyond school libraries and even most public libraries. Everything from the U.S. Library of Congress catalog to the results of ongoing scientific research are on the Net.

The biggest difficulties for children using Net resources is the quantity and level of information. Frankly, unless a child learns how to conduct a search on the Net, he or she will be inundated with material that may or may not relate to the research topic. I've conducted searches that resulted in literally thousands of sources. In addition, much of the material on the Net is for researchers and their students, not for the average elementary or even high-school student. Parents might have to help interpret some of this material (and learn, too). On the Web, though, there is a growing body of lay-oriented information, including everything from government reports to medical information.

"The Web is particularly well-suited for travel-related information, which can turn family vacations into educational experiences."

Because of the Net's global outreach, many cities, countries, states and regions are developing sites that provide information about the people, places and history of geographic areas. Much of this is now indexed in user-friendly directories (see appendix). We've found that because Web sites are typically multi-media (at least nice photos with the text), children like to explore areas they will be visiting. Chambers of commerce are now getting involved in this kind of Web promotion as well, creating many commerce-based pages that provide information about lodging, area attractions, restaurants and the like. You'll have to sift through some of this stuff to get at the more educational pages.

The Internet's World Wide Web has also become a remarkably good place to read current periodicals. I've seen estimates that suggest there are as many as 3,000 periodicals on the Web. I don't know how to assess those kinds of figures, since the periodicals are scattered all over the Net by subject. But there certainly is a plethora of journals and magazines, including many of the popular newsweeklies, newspapers, regional and computer magazines. It's easy to store the addresses for these periodicals in the "bookmark" or "favorite places to go" section of your Web browser, so you can instantly return to the pages of a favorite periodical. Very likely most of these periodicals will at some point start charging subscription fees for online access or will increase the advertising content of the pages. For the time being, though, most periodicals can be easily accessed without expense. This is terrific for students doing current-events research and for all people who would like to know more about the world they inhabit.

I like to think of the Net as a kind of educational flea market. You never quite now what you'll find on a given topic until you run a search through the directories and search engines. The Net is not as well-organized as an encyclopedia, but it's information tends to be richer and certainly more up-do-date. Moreover, at many sites there are listed e-mail addresses for the people in charge. Many of these experts will respond to sincere questions from children and adults. In fact, they're often flattered that anyone cared enough even to ask a question! Unlike traditional reference sources, then, the Net can teach children how to do research by talking via computer with the researchers and experts.

How Can Parents Deal with the Web's Entertainment Deluge?

Family use of the Net, especially the Web, often results in an unbelievable barrage of entertainment possibilities. Perhaps the fastest-growing area on the Web, apart from computer-related topics, is entertainment. Every day the "What's New" listings on the Web include all kinds of new entertainment sites. Not surprisingly, the Web has become one of the major promotional vehicles for the entertainment industry, including music and video clips, samples of computer games, listings of television programs and films, and on and on. If we include "sports" as entertainment, the average person could browse the Web's entertainment sites 24 hours a day and never catch up with the new material being published online every day.

If all of this were not enough, the Web is simply entertaining as a pastime activity. Many people spend hours every day surfing the Net for interesting sites. Since the Web breeds thousands of new pages every day, the "virtual" stream of entertainment is unending. It's safe to say that some people tire of surfing, but for anyone who likes it the supply of new material vastly outstrips what any person could possibly consume. This surfing mentality creates its own drama: anticipation of what will appear next on the screen, what novel sites will be uncovered and what sheer thrills will occur. It's not completely unlike the thrill of watching a soap opera. Indeed, the sex-oriented sites are among the most widely surfed areas.

Parents face a real task in trying to convince their children that surfing is not one of the greatest leisure pursuits. First, parents are responsible for promoting the kind of balanced lives that kids need, including time for interacting with friends, reading, schoolwork, prayer and physical activities. Sometimes children will surf together or with their parents, but generally this does not work well because the one controlling the computer mouse is like the one controlling the television remote control unit.

> **"There's no sense in creating another arena for the kids to fight; if they can't surf together, don't let them surf! It's amazing how this incentive creates more harmonious computer times."**

Second, parents have to encourage creative play that helps youngsters develop their talents and gifts. Along these lines, some parents might find that their visually gifted children really enjoy creating their own Web pages. Believe it or not, this is not particularly difficult, and some Internet access providers also give subscribers free pages for publishing their own material. And these sites can be multi-media, including audio and video sections. There are plenty of sites on the Web on authoring Web documents (look under "HTML" in the "Internet" sections of directories, and see the appendix). You can see the codes used to create any page on the Web by going to the *source* item in the browser menu. Fairly inexpensive graphics programs enable children to design their own home pages. These pages can be viewed in the Web browser even when the computer is not connected to the Net.

Finally, the Net provides some opportunities for turning entertainment interests into an education. There are many Web sites that follow television programs, movies and other entertainment. Sometimes these sites even collect historical and critical information about the stories depicted in dramas and documentaries. The Discovery Channel is a leader in this regard. Historical stories are probably the best for this kind of endeavor, but you might want to try it even with some of the more literate contemporary comedies and dramas. The Net community tends to create its own, critical responses to popular entertainment. In many cases this critical response is educational, not just humorous or entertaining.

The key is whether the site is controlled by the entertainment industry or by fans and critics. The latter groups are more likely to reflect on entertainment, thereby making their entertaining web sites educational.

Should Parents Encourage Budding Net Hackers?

This question has really faced my wife and me. One of our children has been a remarkable computer user for years. Should we have encouraged this ability? Why? Why not?

My gut reaction was always to discourage too much time on the computer. In my view, computers were only worthwhile if they could accomplish something for you, such as composing a letter or creating a graphic for a church bulletin. I always thought in terms of the computer as a means to a given end — like a pencil (who needs to play with a pencil?). Meanwhile, my wife didn't know what to make of our offspring's computer interests; she knew even less about computers than I did.

Well, we now see that we were both ignorant about computers. In some sense a computer *is* like a musical instrument or a sketching pencil. In gifted hands, a computer can create things of beauty, joy and humor. These crazy machines help people to compose messages — visual, aural and literary — as well as to solve mathematical problems. Computers are remarkably versatile instruments, not just cold, dry, dull technologies for drab but necessary human purposes.

Think of all the people who use computers: actuaries, accountants, graphic artists, writers (of many kinds), managers and administrators, teachers and students, editors, reporters, musicians, and on and on and on. Those of us who grew up before the widespread use of computers tend to minimize their significance in all areas of life. Worse than that, we tend to think of computer work as "computer science" or "programming," when in fact computers are used for all kinds of things.

"Computers are indeed like fancy pencils and pens, brushes, musical instruments and video cameras (you can take photos on digital cameras that reproduce the images right on the computer screen!)."

So my answer to the question is a qualified *"yes."* We should encourage our computer-gifted children. We would be remiss not to recognize their abilities and to encourage them to develop those gifts.

But now comes the hard part. *How* and *when* do we encourage such gifts? Is there even some way to distinguish between the computer-addicted geek and the truly gifted child prodigy in computerland? Should the parents simply plow more money into better and better computers?

I like to distinguish between *computer-gifted* and *computer-obsessed* children. They both may seem to be really competent at the keyboard, but the former has his or her life relatively balanced, whereas the latter wakes, eats, plays and sleeps computers. No matter how computer-able the latter is, the obsession is a seed of potential emotional problems and social maladjustments. To the best of my knowledge, no one knows why some kids get so absolutely obsessed with a particular thing, like computers, but the fact is that they do. In my view, the gift is dangerous to a computer-crazed kid whose life is nothing but modems, mice, keyboards and hard drives.

To the computer-obsessed child, the Internet is like the proverbial candy store. Lacking self-control, the kid eats to the point of sickness, then starts it all over again. The Net expands the candy store into a candy factory and a candy mall. It simply is not good for such a child.

I appeal to parents to keep their computer-gifted children on an even keel. Provide equipment and software for them to grow, learn and produce worthwhile things. Even encourage them along the way with appropriate words of praise. I'll go so far as to suggest that you build up their ability in front of their neighbors and friends. In short, let the child know that they have some real talents.

But always stay on the lookout for obsessive behaviors that may signal that the computer gifts are short-circuiting the child's development into a normal, balanced individual. If the child stays up with the computer night after night, you've probably got a problem. If he or she prefers to hack away than play with friends and family, watch out! If the child always talks computers, and seems unable to carry on a decent conversation on another topic or with a person who is computer illiterate, please help the child achieve better balance. All human gifts can turn to obsessions. Alert parents can help prevent this from happening.

The computer-gifted child who is not obsessive can really grow his or her gifts on the Internet. The Net is absolutely loaded with computer news and techniques, along with other computer-gifted people. On the Net a young person can learn much about what other people do with computers for a living. The gifted computer child can also find all kinds of opportunities to create Web pages for Christian organizations and other worthwhile groups. On top of all of that, this type of balanced computer child can meet other, balanced kids, create friendships and exchange what they have each learned.

All of this Net-based computer learning takes place in the context of some of the potential problems I've already discussed. Parents need to be partners in the child's learning, spending time with the child and carefully following their offspring's lives online. Even the nicest and best-adjusted kids can get hurt by other, evil-intentioned computer users when the children leave via modem the relative safety of the home.

Families that Net Together, Grow Together

There are no simple answers to all of the legitimate concerns that parents have about the Net. But since the Internet is not merely a fad, but an ongoing digital revolution in communication, parents will have to address the proper role of the new medium in their homes. Computer-to-computer communication will eventually become quite common in middle- and upper-middle-class homes. Parents may stop thinking very much about it altogether, as often happens with television.

Instead of rejecting the new medium, I think parents will have to let it into the home. All of the educational benefits—the personal joy of e-mail with friends and relatives, the resources for ministry, the sports and entertainment information— will force the issue. And this is not all bad, because there is truly much of value on the Net. Unless families communicate about the Net, however, the children will grow up living in their own Net culture without adequate discernment and balance. The Net is increasingly a public medium, and parents ought to monitor it as much as they would any other public communication that enters the home. More than that, parents ought to look for opportunities for the children to use their gifts and talents in the new medium for the glory of God. Then the kids have learned the Net much like someone learns another language, but with the wisdom necessary to use it in God-pleasing ways.

CHAPTER SEVEN

Publishing Your Own Web Pages
(Dr. Q's Ten Commandments for Effective Web Pages)

One day I was surfing through the "Yahoo" directory on the World Wide Web, noting the usual postings of all kinds of Web pages. Then I hit one that really attracted my attention. It was a listing for "Children" under the heading "Entertainment: People."

For those of you not familiar with the Web, let me point out that the "Entertainment: People" listing in directories is a way for individuals to get their personal home page (the "beginning" spot for an organization or person, like the first page of a book) on the Web. Some of these people are professional entertainers, but the vast majority are common folks who have created more or less entertaining Web sites. What would be on a child's home page?

I surfed to the listing of children, only to have one of the more enjoyable browses on the Net that day. The sites were created by the kids themselves, with all of the innocence, joy and sheer enthusiasm of childhood. The sites included graphics, personal statements about their likes and dislikes, a few humorous photos, poetry, prose and jokes.

> **"If kids can create their own Web pages, so can you — both for yourself and for organizations, including your church, parachurch groups and other Christian ministries."**

You might not create the most artful or aesthetically pleasing pages on the Web, but you can create simple, clean, effective pages that communicate. Web pages are not hard to create. They do require, however, some skill in writing, graphic layout and composition. It also helps to know something about marketing, ethics, communication and, of course, computers. As I suggested in chapter six, constructing Web pages can be both fun and educational. Families can do it together. Ministries can do it to broaden their reach, to increase their impact, to establish new constituencies — simply put, to minister.

Moreover, you don't even have to have access to the Internet's World Wide Web in order to create and view your pages. As long as you have a Web *browser* (the software to surf the Web) on your computer, and at least a simple graphics program, you can create and view the pages on the browser just as they'll look on the Net.

Can You Really Get Your Own Web Pages on the Net?

Absolutely! People do it every day. The Web is not just for highly trained graphic artists and experienced writers or computer aficionados. As many people have pointed out, the Web is "everyone's" publishing medium. Potentially millions of people could see your work, especially if you promote it wisely across the Internet, as I'll discuss shortly.

> **"The Web makes it possible for just about anyone with minimal computer experience to start publishing their own material right on the Internet."**

The first place to consider publishing is on your own access provider's Web server (a computer that "gives" pages to the Web). More and more access providers give one or more free pages on their computer to all of their subscribers. Unfortunately, sometimes they will let you publish pages only in a pre-established format. This makes for a dull, predictable Web site.

Second, try the place where you, a spouse, parent or other close friend works. Some of the kids' Web pages I perused in the "entertainment" directory were placed on Web servers that were owned by their parents' companies, universities and the like. Frequently organizations will let you put your home page on their site (not on the same pages with the business information, of course). But you get your own address (*URL*), which you can give to friends with web browsers who can then "check out" your work. URLs are becoming a status symbol on business cards, just as e-mail addresses were a short while ago.

Third, see if one of the local Internet access providers (see appendix) will sell web pages for a nominal cost. This is increasingly the case, even if you don't have an account with that provider. Even the big, commercial online services are getting into the act. The costs are minimal in most cases.

Fourth, see if you have a local "free net" with open pages that you can use for little or no charge. These community-oriented sites are sometimes run by schools, libraries and other non-profit, educational groups. Frequently they permit residents to publish on their Web sites (see appendix).

Finally, consider getting in the back door by offering to create some Web pages for a local business, church or civic group. Assuming they pay for the "space" on the server, and you do the construction for them, you might be able to persuade the group to give you some of the space for your own, personal home page. It happens all the time. Since you can create the pages on your own computer, you could even create the web pages before showing them to the group. If the group likes the pages, you probably have a job!

How Do You Learn the Basics of Web Construction?

If you're already on the Web, you've got it made. There are wonderful sites that explain and demonstrate how to construct basic and even complicated web pages (see appendix). The Web itself is loaded with free "publications" for novices and veteran surfers. These sites include links to the software tools that might help give your site a professional look (such as tools to remove the "background" to your graphics, so the background seems transparent online). The kind of formatting (the way of creating the page) used on the Web is known as HTML (HyperText Markup Language). You can always use one of the Web search engines to find more information on HTML.

"The formatting used to create Web pages lets you write them with any simple word processor."

You don't even need an expensive, high-power word-processing program (in fact, you're better off not using one, because they sometimes create problems). Some of the major word-processing programs will let you "save" or "convert" documents automatically to HTML, but never without some *bugs* (problems). So you really should know HTML even if you're going to use one of the "conversion" programs for a word processor or graphics program. Essentially, HTML "codes" your text and graphics, turning them into a page when you look at them "through" the Web browser. In your original document, you type in a word, letter or symbol that tells the browser how to "read" your page. For example, if you put an <i> before a sentence, and </i> after the sentence, the browser will read that sentence as italics. The "<>" symbols tell the browser that the "i" is a description tag and not part of the text. The forward-slash symbol (/) merely indicates the end of the "i" (italic). Believe it or not, that kind of simple coding is at the heart of HTML.

For people who are text-oriented, you can also learn the basics of HTML by reading some of the fine books now available even in smaller bookstores. Look under the "computer programming" or "Internet" sections of the store. I'm impressed with the clarity of some of the books, but I've noticed that they often are a bit out of date; they do not always include some of the latest features of HTML, and they miss many of the "tricks of the trade" that are practiced widely on the Web.

Finally, it's essential that you spend time cruising the Net, looking at the codes used to produce the pages that you find interesting. After you find a page that has some features you would like to use in your page, look at the page's "source code," which is nothing less than the actual HTML coding for the page. You can do this by selecting "view source" or an equivalent command from the browser menu. This command gives you the actual coding, which you can then write down, print or save on your computer. You can view the coding for any pages on the Web. By comparing the coding with the actual look of the page, you can figure out how they constructed the page. Assuming you have some of your own graphics, you could construct the same page, substituting your own graphics for those used in the original. This process makes it relatively easy to learn HTML formatting for creating your own Web pages.

What Other Tips Should You Know Before Creating Web Pages?

Well, the most important tips are not technical. There are all kinds of pages on the Web that are expertly crafted from a technical perspective. The biggest problem with most Web pages is that they are simply poor communication. Neither the image nor the text creates a very effective message. In fact, the text and images often say very different things! Each of the following "tips" is designed to help you design effective Web pages.

1. Carefully State the Purpose for the Web Site.

We might as well start at the beginning, where most problems occur in Web-page design. If you don't have a very clear purpose behind the *site* (group of pages), you will likely communicate confusion or silliness to the people who visit your site. There are so many fine specimens of lousy Web pages without purpose or focus that some people have started creating directories of the "worst" sites on the Web. I guess they are trying to move the study of bad art to a new level of humorous kitsch. May you never make it on any of these lists.

"Web pages should be primarily communication, not hot-shot computer technology, fancy graphics or mere information."

Every site should be designed to communicate something specific — to say something in particular, to provide some information in particular, to help someone in a particular way, to notify people of particular events, etc.

Web site design begins, then, with a clear sense of who will use the site, not with a desire to inflate the ego of the person who makes the pages. There are thousands of home pages, in particular, that seem to have been created merely for the amusement of the person whose name is at the top of the page. From a Christian perspective, I'm not so sure that this kind of self-centered Web-site design is very justifiable. Instead, I would encourage you to consider how to help other people by communicating with them. This kind of selfless communication may take many forms, such as encouraging people to sample an inspirational book or video, asking people to call an 800 number to purchase Christian music, inviting people to a convention or conference, making people aware of important information, persuading people to think accurately about your organization, and so forth.

2. Give People Something with Take-Away Value

People who are new to the Web generally don't understand this concept because it comes largely from the so-called "Net Culture" — the dominant values and beliefs among Internet users. Historically the Net was not seen as a commercial communications medium for selling products or even selling Net access. It was a highly non-commercial, largely educational environment dedicated to research and collegiality. Although the dedication to research is not nearly so strong on the Net today, and the users are more representative of the population than the academic community, the "free" mentality still pervades the Net. This is perhaps the major reason why so many companies that try to sell things on the Web fail.

Web users are slowly accepting the commercialization of the Net, but on their own terms. Commercialization is generally acceptable only when it is sought by someone, not when it seeks someone. In other words, it's okay to set up a commercial Web site designed to make money, but don't force other people to see your site. Similarly, *netiquette* emphasizes the importance of sending e-mail only to those who request it, and never sending commercial messages to people who have not requested them (see the appendix for a great netiquette site on the Web). Some of the people who have mistakenly done this have found themselves on the receiving end of thousands of negative messages; in Net jargon, they were *flamed*.

> **"As a general rule, Web sites should be designed with the purpose of giving something to the people who surf the pages."**

It's acceptable to sell products, but don't *merely* sell things; *give* something as well. I like to refer to this as "take-away value," and I consider it quite Christian. Of course products alone can "give" to people; they can meet real needs, satisfy good desires and lead people to holier and more ethical lives. But a Web site that is merely a store, with no apparent take-away value, is likely not to work on the Web. Online catalogs, for instance, are notoriously unsuccessful without something more — something given to the people who browse the catalog.

Years ago I noticed that Land's End, the big mail-order clothing company in Wisconsin, was including things with take-away value in its catalogs. Among the valuable content were some wonderful stories and essays about the history of clothing, fabric, artisans, locations, holidays and the like. Occasionally written by well-known writers, these articles turned Land's End's catalog into a magazine; the company "gave" these articles to its customers, who in turn purchased clothing. Customers learned from the essays, and presumably they found some delight in the writings as well. This is precisely the kind of spirit that works on the Web: give to people, don't just try to take from them. (In my view, this is sensible business practice for any organization.)

If you don't have anything to give people who come by your pages, you should create something. It could be as simple as some excellent graphics composed with precision, high aesthetic values and great creativity (sounds like art, eh?). Or it could be as complicated as a collection of the latest research on archeology of the Holy Land. Whatever it is that you are giving, however, it should relate to the first point above — the overall purpose for the site. In other words, if you are selling church clip art, you ought to be able to give some superb samples of church clip art. Similarly, if your site is meant to encourage people to buy a book that will help improve their marriages, then you ought to be able to give them something that will help their marriage, such as a sample chapter from the book!

Think creatively about the value you intend to give people to take away with them. One of the most important and sadly lacking things on the Net is easy means of finding information on particular topics. There are many directories, but there are needs for many more of them, particularly specialized directories. When we began developing the Gospel Films site at the Gospel Communications Network, we discovered that there were no Web directories of sites related to Christians in professional and collegiate sports. Given Gospel Films president Billy Zeoli's longstanding involvement in professional sports chapels, this seemed a natural ministry opportunity. Consequently, we began compiling such a directory, even to the point of contacting Christian athletic organizations and offering to give them space at the site. We also created an *e-zine* (Net lingo for an online magazine) which updated readers on the Christian sports scene around the world. Of course Gospel Films sells and rents sports-related videos, such as the fine Dave Dravecky video (*Dravecky: A Story of Courage and Grace*), and we linked the news site to the video catalog. But our goal at the magazine was never principally to sell the videos, but to encourage and inform people about the ways that Christ is alive in sports via Christian sports athletes. We believed that such stories could inspire, encourage, uplift and even lead people to Christ.

"Promotions are very important on the Net because they help bring attention to sites and encourage people to check out a particular page, but the ones that are most effective have take-away value."

If your personal or organizational goal on the Web is to sell something, don't forget this principle. Look for promotions that will give people "money off," complimentary products, helpful catalogs, and so forth. The Gospel Communications Network's excellent graphic designer, Warren Kramer, once showed me some of his terrific, full-color scenes of God's Creation of the universe. They are artistic renderings, of course, based on Warren's imagination as well as his understanding of the Scriptures. Someone at Gospel Films realized that they would make wonderful scenes for a computer screen saver. Before long, the screen-saver project was completed, and Gospel Films was offering on the Net the high-quality screen saver free to anyone who purchased one of their videos. We were pleased that God used Warren's gifts for the benefit of the wider Christian computer-using community.

What do you have to give to other people? How can you help the Christian or non-Christian Web community? Of course, we can all share the Gospel, and I hope that many Web sites will do that directly and unashamedly. But what about other, day-to-day needs and concerns? What about peoples' love of stories, including novels and short stories, and even jokes (Hey, how about a Christian humor site, focusing on real stories about funny things that happened in church?; check out the GCN home page (http://www.gospelcom.net) to see if we got this launched. If not, launch it!). Giving to others is Christian. It also makes very good sense on the Net.

3. Make Every Part of Your Site High-Concept

I haven't figured out all of the reasons for this, but the fact is that the multi-media Web is essentially a medium for high-concept communication. Like a good speech or a fine advertisement, it's a medium of theme or concept. Densely thick pages simply don't communicate effectively. Neither do unorganized pages lacking unity and focus. The best Web sites, even the best single pages, have one, clear idea that drives the rest of the site.

Sometimes Web gurus refer to this as specialization. They argue that because there is so much material on the Web, let alone the entire Net, people will focus only on pages that are directed at their particular interests. I don't think that specialization is the best way of looking at communication on the Web.

I prefer *high-concept*, which describes the best sites regardless of how specialized they are. Some of the most popular sites on the Web, such as *Wired* magazine, are not really specialized. Instead, they offer particular information and a kind of online atmosphere or mind-set — a concept.

The Bible Gateway is a perfect example. All kinds of people from all over the world turn to the Gateway to get the Scriptures in a variety of languages. In fact, the Gateway is linked to probably thousands of Web pages that use it for Scripture references. But when you go to the Bible Gateway, you know exactly what you are getting. The concept is simple: the Scriptures in multiple languages. Period. No novels about the scriptures, no graphical depictions of Bible stories — just the Scriptures in many "tongues." The concept is simple: one place on the Web for Scriptures in all tongues. That's about as High of a concept as you can get (sorry, I couldn't resist the pun).

"The most successful commercial and ministry Web sites are high-concept."

They don't just sell coffee, they sell a concept related to coffee: relaxation, enjoyment, collegiality, and so forth. When you enter some of the coffee sites, the pages virtually smell like breakfast in the nook overlooking the lake. Coffee could also be approached as "quality" or "variety" or "exotic"; there are always variations on a high-concept theme.

As Christian publishers take to the Web, I wonder what they will do regarding concept. Will they approach their pages in terms of high-concept, such as "integrity" or "quality," or will they simply create enormous, seemingly unending pages of catalog material that creates a jumbled mess in the minds of Net users?

Clearly the notion of high-concept is fraught with potential ethical dilemmas. Christians ought to consider whether or not their Web concepts mirror reality. Truth is sometimes stretched even in Christian publishing. The publishers that have a clear sense of their calling within the Kingdom are in a better position to launch successful Web pages.

Finally, the idea of high-concept makes it far easier to promote sites on the Web. Without clear concepts, Web sites will not be as rich for cross-promotion in a variety of directories and under numerous topics. A Christian youth ministry, for instance, that focuses on providing resources, not just on the general concept of ministry, can be promoted under the relevant "non-Christian" directories, such as "educational video" or "youth-culture resources." Concept drives promotion by bridging distinctly Christian sites to the broader culture. Without a high concept, sites tend to get lost in the Web shuffle; they lack memorable, focused appeal.

4. Set a Limit on Per-Page Data

The Web is a terrific digital medium for multi-media communication, but it has its limits, especially speed. The technology permits much quicker communication that most people are able to achieve. Unfortunately, many people design pages under false assumptions about the speed at which the users are able to access the text and especially the graphics. It is essential to design your site for the average user, since there are an awful lot of them compared to a few privileged people who can operate near the technological limit.

> ## "In the foreseeable future, modem speeds, more than any other technology, should dictate the amount of material that you put on any one Web page."

Since most people on the Web are using regular telephone modems, we should design our sites accordingly. My experience suggests some rather specific parameters for normal page design. If your entire file of graphics and text for a particular page is greater than about 70,000 bytes (70K), then you are really expecting users to wait patiently for your pages to download from the *serving* computer to the user's *client* computer. More data than 70K per page simply doesn't make a lot of sense for most Web construction. You can check in your graphics and text software to see how big your Web files are. I would normally keep pages at less than 70K.

There are exceptions. One is Web sites that are intended merely to be showcases for spectacular graphics and other features. People will wait for something especially great or unusual, but generally only if they know that it is truly special. Another exception is some of the multimedia work that makes extensive use of audio and video. Most people who try to download audio and video files know that it is going to take a while. For instance, some of the audio I download takes about three times longer to download than it does to play the audio clip. Fortunately the new *streaming* audio and video files are not a problem because they send the files to the user in more or less real time, permitting the user to listen to or view the material as it is being downloaded. But if you cannot use the streaming technology, you should tell the user on your web site how large the audio or video file is and about how long it will take to download it at normal Net speeds.

How many pages of "raw" text are too many? People talk on the Web about home pages, but the fact is that most pages are longer than two standard computer screens or one full-size piece of paper. I've seen as much as forty pages of text in one Web page. And that forty pages downloaded quite quickly because it was all text. In this type of situation the limits on data are not total data, but reader fatigue and frustration. If someone is looking for something fairly specific on the page, they don't want to wade through forty pages. Normally we should divide more than about two pages of text into shorter sections, organizing them by topics or questions. Use the basic *tree* model that goes from broad subjects and topics to increasingly specialized or selective ones, with hypermedia links for each transition.

5. Mix and Match Media

Many people are attracted to the Web because of its multi-media character — text, still image, moving image and sound. But the two dominant media for now are text and still image, including photographs and drawings. Just as variety is a good working principle in aesthetics, the best Web sites mix and match text with illustrations. Sites that are either too graphic-intensive or too text-intensive lack such richness.

Even some of the top corporations don't seem to understand this fundamental principle. Their graphic artists seem to go wild, creating elaborate visual renditions on the home page. Three pages later in the same site, everything is layers of text. What happened? Did the company run out of site-construction funds or did the designers go on vacation? And why didn't the writers argue for more text in the first few pages of material? I don't know how this happens, but it does.

> **"The best Web sites balance visual emphasis and textual content through all of the pages."**

Often there is more graphic emphasis at the beginning or "top" of every page, but at least some graphics continue through each section of the site. In the truly inspired sites, the graphics enhance the specific textual content. In this regard, I'd like to offer kudos to the gang at the Gospel Communications Network, which has consistently applied this principle among its many ministries (see appendix). They have wonderfully balanced sites with enough visual content to make the pages interesting, but not enough to turn the sites into glitzy goulash. They also use graphics and audio or video that support the image and the real ministry purpose of each site.

6. Make Each Page as Interactive as Possible

Perhaps the most significant difference between the Net's World Wide Web and other media is interactivity. The Web is like remote-control television, but even more interactive. Instead of selecting from among only a few channels, users of the Web select from millions of pages of material. More than that, they select from among the options on each page, including video, audio, text and image. With most browsers, users can decide in advance if they want any images; they can surf around the Net looking only at text until they decide to request information in any other form. If all of that were not enough interactivity, they can also send messages to people, enter online contests, order products, search the Web for key subjects and persons, and so forth. By its very nature, the Web is highly interactive for the individual user. Web-site designers need to take this into account for successful pages.

> ## "One way of understanding this interactivity is to focus on the non-linear way that the Web organizes communication."

Textbooks are largely linear; they organize information in sequential order by chapters and sub-sections. The reader of a text assumes that the content builds on itself, thereby negating the value of beginning with the middle chapter or the last chapter. The Web follows "horizontal" paths as well; a particular hypertext link might take you to an in-depth exploration of *a related* topic, not to a deeper exploration of the initial topic at hand.

For instance, you might discover at a page on the topic of "sports" a link for any of the following: names of athletes, individual sports such as tennis or golf, sports teams and organizations, and so on. If you go to the link of a sports person's name, you are likely to find there things that don't have anything directly to do with sports, such as links to the sports person's family or town.

These are horizontal links that delve into other, related subjects, not just deeper into the initial subject. The best Web sites are scattered with these kinds of interactive links, because the creator of the Web pages can never be absolutely sure what the user is looking for in the first place.

If you were a Christian book publisher, how would you make the pages about a particular new book as interactive as possible? Well, let's assume that the purpose of the site is to inform people not only of the availability of the book, but of the *theme* of the book. Anything that would help communicate that theme effectively could be a worthwhile link. This might include an interactive interview with the author, excerpts from book reviews or commendations, excerpts from the book itself, an audio clip of the author speaking on the topic of the book, and so on.

"Another way of thinking about the Web's interactivity is the high degree of user control."

Unlike broadcasting, for instance, which essentially presents the programs in specified form, the Web lets the user create the messages through a series of interactive choices. Two individuals may enter the same Web site at the same time, but they could then "visit" very different parts of that site in a widely different sequence and for contrasting lengths of time. When users feel like they lack such options on the Web, they will not likely stay at a site very long — unless they are extremely interested in the material published at the site.

The best Web sites, then, anticipate some of the needs or interests of the users, creating optional links that help them pursue their own particular interests. This means that sites should include many internal links across the pages (e.g., a video catalog site should permit users to link to video subjects and video uses, such as educational vs. recreational, and to information about the people in the videos or the people or companies that made them). The site should also link to ideas about how to use the videos most effectively, links to what others have said about the value or quality of the videos. Also, the best sites anticipate user interests by providing links to external pages at other sites.

Consider how one should construct an online interview. The worst thing you could do would be simply to publish the straight text of the interview, perhaps 20 pages. With no links, and with 20 pages of "linear" material, the site would not be accessed for long by most people, who would rapidly become frustrated with the chore of reading screen after screen of text on their computer monitors. Of course, you could spice up the pages a bit by adding some graphics, including photos, but this is a poor solution, since download time will increase rapidly.

Instead, why not use each interview question as a hypertext link? Users could quickly scan down the page, reading all of the questions, and deciding which questions they are most interested in pursuing; in effect, they can create their own interview out of the existing one (the first chapter of this book, a series of questions and answers about the Net, is available online in exactly this form — including new questions and answers added all the time; you can visit this "virtual appendix" at the URL given in the appendix to this book). Moreover, each answer page could include some simple, fast-loading graphics, such as a one-color line drawing of the interviewee answering that question (this graphic could even be the background for the text answer). Graphics could be added to the question page as well, of course. And a few audio clips for several of the answers could be provided as options instead of the text responses. Indeed, a few video clips might work very well for users who have fast modems and are really interested in seeing the interviewee respond to a particular question — but only with the option of text, first.

"Christian Web publishers should consider the potential of interactivity to contribute to the overall goals of their sites."

For instance, if the site is intended to teach about God's word, all references to the scriptures should be hypertext links to the actual Bible passages, with opportunities for the user to select larger portions of scripture (assuming he or she might not be familiar with those passages, and would like some context). This is easily accomplished through the Bible Gateway, which provides scriptures in multiple languages for linking (see appendix). Similarly, suppose the purpose of a site is to help youth ministers do their work more effectively. If there are pages on the Web that offer additional, related information, your site should include them as hypertext links. Similarly, if particular topics of information have already been covered in the youth-ministry site, you should provide an interactive means for users to access that older material. If the information could be communicated significantly better with examples or illustrations, these should be provided, perhaps in another medium (e.g., audio or video).

While surfing through one of the directories to Christian material on the Web, I ran across an amazing example of successful interactivity. The particular "page" was an essay by the Pope on the importance of the church's use of new media technologies. Every footnote in the essay was a hypertext link to the full text of the footnoted article! Could you imagine how this kind of linkage would change research and writing?

7. Personalize the Web Site

In spite of the cold, digital way that the Net transmits information, it can be a remarkably personal medium. The Web, in particular, with its multi-media opportunities, is able to create a sense of personal communication between users and the people who run Web sites. The Web is inherently person-to-person communication; it's the interaction between the individual computer user and the person or persons represented on the Web pages. Sometimes I like the metaphor of the telephone conversation to get this point across to people. The phone is merely wires and electronics, and the people may be thousands of miles apart, but the conversation is remarkably personal.

The Web is not as personal as telephone dialogue, but it is nonetheless a medium that thrives on personalized communication. In my view, this puts corporate communication at an immediate disadvantage, since large organizations never speak with the same personal voice as individuals (even if they have similar legal rights). On the other hand, it gives individual communicators, such as artists, a powerful medium to communicate directly with their audiences. It also offers a means for small-scale entrepreneurs to personalize their relationships with customers. In ministry, the Web permits the closest thing to direct ministry of any of the major mass media, precisely because the Web is not a particularly mass medium.

"Unfortunately, personalization can be enormously unethical."

As in some forms of television preaching, where the televangelist misrepresents his "personal" relationship with the viewing audience, the Web can be used wrongly to generate artificial relationships that enable Web publishers to take advantage of Web users. I am not speaking in support of this kind of lamentable activity, which is already developing on the Web among some so-called "ministries." Personalized communication, whenever it is not grounded in real, local relationships, can easily be misused for the selfish benefit of a person or institution.

Instead, I am talking about legitimate communication in which a person or organization is trying to explain who or what they really are.

Consider these possibilities:

1. The Christian author who uses the Web to create a multimedia arena expressing his or her major writing ideas and themes, as well as personal reflections about the process of writing,

2. The Christian musician who uses the Web to reveal the worldview and personal convictions behind the music,

3. The Christian church that uses the Web to interpret for non-members what it believes, who it seeks to serve, and how it conducts ministry,

4. The Christian periodical that uses the Web as a forum for readers to interact with its writers and editors, thereby clarifying the values and convictions that drive the periodical's decision making,

5. The Christian missions organization that offers Web users a glimpse into the process of training and supporting missionaries, as well as a peek at the results of such missions work.

All of these can be very legitimate uses of the Web to establish authentic communication between Christian individuals and organizations, on the one hand, and the Web users, on the other.

I strongly encourage Web-site designers and the people and institutions that they serve to personalize their presence on the Net. Let people know who you are, what you believe, and why you're working in cyberspace. Contrasted with so much of the false personalization on the Net, including the widespread use of fictitious names and artificially inflated rhetoric, this authentic presence would bring salt and light to cyberspace. Why should we be afraid to tell people who we really are, why we care about Jesus Christ, and why we are motivated to get on the Net? The only answer I can offer is that we are not settled enough in our own faith to let others know who we really are. In this case, I think it's safe to say that the best Christian groups to publish in Web sites are those that have a clear sense of their calling, their gifts and their fallenness. The fear of God itself ought to be enough to keep people from misrepresenting themselves.

8. Include Changing *(Virtual)* Sections of Pages and Sites

I don't think this requires an awful lot of explanation. Too many sites are constructed once and never changed. They include nothing that would encourage people to return to the site, to dig deeper into the site, or to anticipate anything worthwhile in the future for the site. They are static, non-virtual sites and pages that implicitly suggest no relationship between the users and the Web designers and authors.

I understand how this happens: Organizations get excited about the new medium and decide to launch a Net presence. Once the work is underway, some of the disillusionment begins to set in; it's not easy to create high-quality Web sites, especially as part-time work for little or no pay. The only important goal is getting the site done, and by then people are too tired of the whole process to design into the site continual updates, expansion and improvement. Worse yet, funds dry up and the site rests on the Net like a half-finished suburban home with mediocre landscaping that never changes. The site grows old and loses a lot of its earlier appeal. Believe it or not, this is exactly what happens with many corporate sites and personal home pages. After the initial unveiling, there's nothing left to consider.

Perhaps I'm being too hard on Web designers. In one sense, every site is an entity unto itself, just like a completed book or recording. But in a broader sense, this kind of static approach to the Net overlooks some of the potential in the medium. Because the Web is virtual, it can be changed at will. As the technology improves, as the design abilities grow, as the artistic vision is clarified, and especially as the communication purpose is refined, the Web site can serve many more people far more effectively. If anything, the Web is a place where trial and error should be expected and encouraged, and where quality is continually increased.

> **"The ongoing problem facing Web-site designers, then, is not simply how to increase the amount of material on a Web site or on a particular page, but how to regularly update the communication that takes place at the site."**

In some cases this may mean simply that directories are expanded, that more pages are added, or that more timely information is provided. But in some cases the changes will be the result of a desire to make the site more user-friendly, to enhance its visual appeal, to make it more interactive, and the like. The Web practically demands this kind of dynamic approach to communication. As long as there is a good purpose to the change, the dynamism can be pleasing to God and helpful to users.

9. Create a Unified Visual Identity Across All of the Site's Pages

When people not trained in the principles of visual design first begin putting material on the Web, they almost invariably create an optic hodgepodge. In fact, this is such a problem with some Web sites that users forget what site they are at while browsing through multiple pages. I've seen wonderful, even stunning graphics at sites, but the images conflicted with the images on other pages of the same site. In the worst cases, the images even conflicted with the text on the same pages. One was celebratory, for instance, and the other solemn.

> **"Web-site construction is an art, not a science, and the principle of *visual unity* is too important to ignore."**

Once you've decided on the basic purpose of the site — what you're trying to communicate, to whom, why, etc.— you should create a visual concept that supports that purpose. Then the goal is to maintain that visual message across all of the pages of the site, creating variations on the visual theme that provide variety but also maintain unity. The best sites often do this so subtlety that as a user you don't even think about the "identity" of the site; you just "feel" it.

Clean, simple graphics can accomplish this unity far more easily than fancy graphics. Visual simplicity connotes a single concept, one message, one idea. They can use similar or the same icons through the pages, a common background color or texture, particular fonts, and so forth. Elaborate graphics often suggest multiple meanings and conflicting messages. Consequently, the best sites carry through to every page the simple visual concept, adjusting the specific expression of that concept to fit the overall textual message of each section of the site.

10. Promote the Site Online *and* in Other Media

It doesn't make an awful lot of sense to spend time and money creating a wonderful Web site without telling others that the site exists. In addition to promoting the site online, through the usual directories and "what's new" lists (see appendix), it is essential to promote the site in all other accessible media. If it's a personal home page, you might not do much more than tell friends and co-workers to "check out" your page. In most cases, however, organizationally supported sites should be widely cross-promoted in other mass and interpersonal media. This is not simply a matter of prestige or ego ("Hey, guess what *I've* got? My *own* home page!" or "Hey, check out what *my* ministry has! Its very own home page!"). Who really cares? The more important issue is what's on the home pages.

The typical Christian organization should consider cross-promotion in all of the following media:

1. Paper newsletters and correspondence (the URL and e-mail addresses should be printed on these materials),

2. Catalogs, resource pamphlets and brochures,

3. Convention and conference promotional mailings and announcements,

4. Press releases,

5. Business cards of all employees,

6. Broadcast programs, including radio and television spots and shows (give the URL at the end of every broadcast: "Visit our pages on the Internet's World Wide Web at....," or "For more

information about this ministry, please point your Internet Web browsers to...."),

7. Premiums and "thank-you" gifts, such as books and videos,

8. Media interviews (give reporters the URL and ask them to include it in articles as well as to use it for their own research about the ministry, and mention it during live and recorded radio and television programs),

9. Your own products, especially paper products such as audio CD notes and book pages. Examine all of the communication media that your organization uses, and put the URL in every one of them. Don't worry about a change in your URL at a later date; you can "forward" people to the new URL online, just as a telephone number change is announced in a recording to people who call the old number.

"Without significant cross-promotion, your Web work is confined largely to the existing pass-through traffic on the Net."

No doubt you will gain supporters, prayer partners and customers simply by putting your organization on the Net, but the greater benefits come when you tell existing friends and constituency that you are now online. Some of them will get on the Net for the first time just to see and read your material. Others, who have been on the Net but didn't know that your organization was online, will surf to your site to see what you're up to. Before long, you'll have champions of your work, encouraging you with supportive e-mail and perhaps even financial gifts. There's no sense in being in Web-related ministry without communicating about your work. The better the promotion, the more people you will have both to minister to and to pray and support your efforts.

Web Publishing as Vocation

The Internet's World Wide Web is another opportunity for ministry in the widest possible sense. Unlike many other media, however, it's relatively inexpensive and remarkably easy. If young children can design their own Web pages, certainly Christian periodicals, artists, evangelistic ministries, seminaries, publishing houses, youth ministries, Bible-teaching organizations and everyone else can do it as well. Our goal should be to identify the people with the right combinations of gifts — people who can write, design, network and all of the other activities necessary. Above all, we need gifted communicators who can keep focused the church's Web activities, so technology and graphics don't get in the way of effective presentation of high-concept ideas, particularly the highest concept of all — the Gospel of Jesus Christ.

The ideas developed in this chapter are taken from my own experiences consulting with organizations and individuals getting on the World Wide Web. The Gospel Communications Network, in particular, was a fertile ground to test various types of Web-site design in the context of communicating particular messages for effective ministry. I thank GCN and its wonderfully gifted alliance of ministries, all dedicated to serving the Risen Lord through the new medium of digital communication.

To Him be all glory.

APPENDIX

A Christian's Guide to Essential Resources on and about the Net

or Resources for Fishers of the Net: A Personal Tour

Welcome to the revised edition of what might be the first Christian book with a "Virtual Appendix." By the time the revised version of this book went to press, some of the material in the first version of the appendix was already out of date. Such is the way of the Internet, which changes every day. So I created an online version of this appendix that I can update as needed. For the latest appendix, point your Web browsers to this URL (address):

http://www.gospelcom.net/ifc

You can also subscribe free to the e-mail version of my Internet for Christians Newsletter.

Send your message to: **ifc-request@gospelcom.net**

Include only the following message in your note:

SUBSCRIBE your e-mail address
e.g., SUBSCRIBE schu@gospelcom.net

The newsletter is open to anyone, so feel free to tell your friends about it. Once you get on the Web, please drop by to visit the Virtual Appendix.

The Virtual Appendix is merging with CrossSearch, a massive on-line directory to Christian resources on the Net. Visit CrossSearch at:

http://www.crosssearch.com

Internet Resources

Here are some great places to begin your trek up the mountain of Internet lingo and technology.

http://www.yahoo.com/Computers/Internet/

The above site includes many links to help beginners — everything from FAQs (frequently asked questions), to self-guided tours of the Net, dictionaries of Net lingo, how to use e-mail, etc. If you're interested just in information about the World Wide Web, including authoring your own Web pages, here's the place to begin:

http://www.yahoo.com/Computers/World_Wide_Web/

Remember to type these addresses into your Web browser exactly as they are given here. Even the blank spaces have to be underscores, and the slashes are forward slashes, not backward slashes.

If you'd like a guide to using e-mail, this site includes wonderful information by Kaitlin Duck Sherwood:

http:www.webfoot.com/advice/email.top.html

And for a glossary of Internet terms, you'll do well with Matisse Enzer's at:

http://www.matisse.net/files/glossary.html

Don't forget to give some time to learning Net manners (netiquette). For a wonderfully direct and easy to understand guide, see Arlene Rinaldi's "I'm NOT Miss Manner's of the Internet" at:

http://www.fau.edu/rinaldi/netiquette.html

How Do I Get Hooked Up?

The following companies have Internet connectivity with a local phone call in much of the United States:

CompuServe Call: 1-800-848-8199

CompuServe has very competitive pricing and covers about 90% of the U.S. The company is also quite active internationally — more than either Prodigy or America Online. CompuServe has the best online information service among the three as well. Its religious material on its own system includes the Christian Interactive Network and the developing Religious Village. CompuServe also has a service called Spryte that provides only Internet access (not CompuServe's own online material). At the time of revising this appendix, you could get via Spryte unlimited access to the Internet for about $20 U.S. monthly.

America Online Call: 1-800-827-6364

AOL, as it's commonly called, really made its push with easy e-mail access for people in North America. It's a user-friendly system, but not as information-rich as CompuServe. It includes the "Christianity Online" service — another facet of the ever-expanding Christianity Today, Inc. AOL also has the Global Network Navigator (GNN) service for those who wish Internet access only.

Microsoft Network: 1-800-386-5550

It took the "Big M" a while to get on the Internet bandwagon, but now they are rolling with service and their own Web browser for Windows™, Windows95™ and Macintosh.

Prodigy Call: 1-800-PRODIGY

What can you say, except that Prodigy beat the other commercial online services with Web access. Unfortunately, Prodigy's Web browser is slow and not as fully featured as others. Nevertheless, you might find this service does what you need.

AlterNet (UUNET Technologies) Call: 1-800-4UUNET4

This company is known for its high-quality, reliable Internet connectivity. If all you want is the Internet, see if AlterNet is available in your area. AlterNet is increasingly international, too.

NETCOM Call: 1-800-353-6600

NetCom has competitive pricing and good software for cruising the Net with Windows™ and Macintosh. Many beginners rave about the ease of use.

LONG-DISTANCE PHONE COMPANIES

The long-distance phone companies are gearing up for being competitive players in the Internet-access game. Call your long-distance company and see what kind of Internet connectivity rates they quote you.

FREENETS

You might be able to get free Internet access (no joke). These "free nets" are located around the United States. You or a friend can get access to lists of them at the following Web site:

http://www.yahoo.com/Business_and_Economy/Companies/ Computers/Networking/Online_Services/Free_Nets/Free_Nets

LOCAL INTERNET ACCESS PROVIDERS

Also, if you want to check on the Web for the availability of local Internet providers in your area or in a friend's area, go to the following page:

http://www.yahoo.com/Business/Corporations/Internet_ Access_Providers/

INTERNATIONAL ACCESS PROVIDERS

International access information is provided at these sites:

http://www.best.be/iap.html
http://www.netusa.net/ISP/
http://thelist.com/

How Can I Find Christian Stuff on the Net?

One of the best, award-winning sites is the Gospel Communications Network (GCN). Start with any one of the URLs (addresses at GCN) and work your way back to the home page after a grand tour, always "recycling" your browser back through the "GCN Home" buttons on the bottom of the home pages of each one of the sites. There are more than twenty ministries at GCN, including Gospel Films, InterVarsity Christian Fellowship and InterVarsity Press, Radio Bible Class (including *Our Daily Bread* devotional), the Bible Gateway (the Bible in multiple languages and translations, fully searchable), Renewing Your Mind with R.C. Sproul, Children's Bible Hour, Youth for Christ, the International Bible Society, Youth Specialties (check out their "mall"), Ron Hutchcraft Ministries, Words of Hope, Navigators, Reverend Fun (the first online Christian cartoon), my own Internet for Christians site and much more. The URL is:

http://www.gospelcom.net

How Can I Find More Christian Material?

The first places to go are religion or Christian directories. There are many of them, and each one is a bit different. You'll need to spend some time with each one to get a feel for its own "personality." Unfortunately, most of these directories don't have "what's new" sections that you can use effectively to find the latest Christian resources. You'll need to review them every now and then. One major exception is:

CrossSearch

http://www.crosssearch.com
This is one of the most comprehensive and certainly user-friendly directories to Christian resources. It is fully searchable by key words, so you can find exactly what you're looking for. I highly recommend it.

Yahoo's "Christianity" Listing

http://www.yahoo.com/Society_and_Culture/Religion/
Christianity

This is a massive, eclectic directory.

TradeWave Galaxy's "Religion" Listing

http://www.einet.net/galaxy/Humanities/Religion.html

TradeWave is one of the other big directories, and its religious listing is fairly good. Located under "Humanities," though, and not confined to Christian materials, it takes a few more deep breaths to get through in one sitting. You'll get a peek at some of the religious hocus pocus that's on the Web, too.

The Christian Theology Page

http://apu.edu:80/~bstone/theology/theology.html

Brian Stone's directory is amazingly helpful. It includes not just major theological sites around the world, but also listings by Christian tradition.

Theology on the Web

http://wwwvpm.com/thawes/

Another general directory to Christian theology on the Web.

How Do I Find People on the Net?

As I explained in the book, this is one of the toughest things to do. There are no central directories of everyone's e-mail address, although you can bet some company is working on developing one to sell. These resources will take you about as far as you can easily search for someone. See the *Internet for Christians* book for other means of searching. If the person you are looking for has a own home page on the WWW, use one of the search engines in the next section.

Four11 White Page Directory

http://www.four11.com/

This is one of the largest e-mail address listings on the WWW, with millions of peoples' addresses included and searchable by name.

Internet Address Finder

http://www.iaf.net

This site claims to be "the largest white pages service on the Internet." It lets you hunt for a person's e-mail address by organization as well as by name.

E-Mail Address Finding "Tools"

http://twod.med.harvard.edu/labgc/roth/Emailsearch.html

Folks at Harvard are nice enough to provide this useful directory with links to the major "tools" for finding the e-mail addresses of people. None of these tools is comprehensive, but they're the best we've got going.

White NetPages

http://www.aldea.com/whitepages/white.html

This site includes only volunteered e-mail addresses.

Christian Reformed Church Email Addresses

http://www.crcna.org/

Christian Connection (TCM)

http://tcm.nbs.net/~cc/cchome.html

Links to lists of e-mail addresses of Lutherans from the Evangelical Lutheran Church of America, Missouri Synod and Canadian Lutherans. Presbyterian Church in America (PCA) E-Mail Service http://www.usit.net/public/capo/pca/pcaemail.html

How Do I Find Organizations' E-mail Addresses?

E-Mail Directory to Christian Organizations

gopher://una.hh.lib.umich.edu:70/00/inetdirsstacks/
christian%3akreitz

A remarkably eclectic listing of Christian organizations' addresses and e-mail contacts, including everything from bookstores to camps, churches, magazines, cult ministries, and communications ministries.

Christian Connection (TCM)

http://tcm.nbs.net/~cc/cchome.html

All kinds of links to Lutheran organizations — and more.

Yahoo's Directory of Web Search Tools

http://www.yahoo.com/Reference/Searching_the_Web/

What can I say? Yahoo, once again! Be wise, though, some of the search tools listed there are not easy to use.

WebCrawler

http://www.webcrawler.com

This baby really creeps and crawls around the Web, uncovering far more "bugs" than you're probably ready for at this stage. But give it a try.

Lycos

http://www.lycos.com

Carnegie Mellon must have a massive computer for this puppy, because it really searches. If Lycos' full search doesn't find your organization, it's probably not on the Web or the rest of the Net.

Excite

http://www.excite.com

This celebrated newcomer finds what you're looking for fast.

HotBot

http://www.hotbot.com/index.html

Another newbie, HotBot claims to be the fastest and most comprehensive search vehicle.

A List of Search Engines for the Web

http://cuiwww.unige.ch/meta-index.html

InfoSeek

http://www.infoseek.com:80/Home

One of the best search engines for people and organizations on the Net (and for much more) is InfoSeek, a newer, commercial service that also lets you do a number of searches for free. World Council of Churches

How Do I Find Organizations and Other Materials?

It's not hard to find online organizations and other materials. Start at the CrossSearch Directory, using its online search feature that scans through the directory for you. Then use some of the search "engines" listed in this section of this appendix. Along the way try some of the specialized directories listed below:

CrossSearch

http://www.crosssearch.com

A massive directory to Christian online resources that includes a search engine.

AltaVista

http://www.altavista.digital.com

At the time this book went to press, this was the best overall search engine on the Web. It's so good, in fact, that you had better take some time to learn how to narrow your search or you'll end up with far too many "hits" (documents with the word or phrase you seek).

WebCrawler

http://www.webcrawler.com

This baby really creeps and crawls around the Web, uncovering far more "bugs" than you're probably ready for at this stage. But give it a try.

Lycos

http://www.lycos.com

Another superb search engine that includes millions of WWW pages.

InfoSeek

http://www.infoseek.com

This one includes searching beyond the confines of the WWW, especially with the "professional" subscription.

What Are Net Regulations Around the World?

The Net is loaded with international material, but there are some sites that might be particularly helpful. For Internet access, go back to the section on access providers. Here's a useful site for regulatory information:

Yahoo's Directory to Telecommunications Policy Around the World

http://www.yahoo.com/Government/Technology_Policy/ Information_Technology

This will help you and your friends track developments in other countries, including regulation.

How Can I Publicize My Own Web Site?

I have to admit that most Christian Web sites are simply under-publicized, resulting usually in little traffic and little ministry impact. If you are responsible for a Web site, please publicize it adequately.

CrossSearch

http://www.crosssearch.com

Start by submitting your Web site's URL and description to this Christian directory, where it will quickly be picked up by others as well.

Submit It

http://www.submit-it.com

This wonderful Web site has links to all of the major directories and search engines. You can post info about your Web site to all kinds of places on the Web, guaranteeing considerable publicity.

Mailing Lists

What Are Mailing Lists? How Do I Subscribe?

Mailing lists are e-mail "distribution" lists. They are also called listservs and majordomos. These lists enable a person or organization to distribute e-mail automatically to everyone on the list. Normally they permit any list subscriber to send e-mail to everyone else on the list. The best mailing lists are topic-specific; they attract subscribers who are all interested in the subject discussed on the list. The vast majority are free of charge.

They are like "virtual discussions" that take place entirely through e-mail. For instance, suppose I send a message to the list address. As a subscriber, you receive my message and send a response to the list; your response, in turn, is distributed automatically to everyone on the list. Pretty soon a dozen or more people are sending messages about the original topic or question that I "posted." All of those messages are sent to everyone on the list in the order that they were sent to the list address.

There are moderated and unmoderated lists. Unmoderated lists automatically distribute every message to everyone on the list. Moderated lists require all messages to go through one person — the moderator — who decides which messages are worth passing on to the entire group, and which messages should be combined into one message (e.g., one message each day that summarizes or "digests" all of the messages that the moderator received that day).

There are also one-way lists, which permit an organization to send messages to all subscribers, but don't permit other subscribers to do so. These lists function more or less like organizational newsletters. They can save an organization a tremendous amount of time and money compared with sending paper newsletters and faxes.

Mailing lists are easy to use, but you need to keep in mind one major distinction: the difference between subscribing (or unsubscribing) to a list and posting a message to the list. Subscribing and posting require two different messages sent to two different e-mail addresses. Subscriptions normally are handled automatically; you send your request to a computer that automatically subscribes you to the list. When you want to post a message to the list, you send it to a different address — the actual list address. Thus, you need to know two separate addresses — one to subscribe (and unsubscribe) and another to post messages. Incidentally, when you subscribe to a list you'll receive a "form" message telling you that you are subscribed, explaining how to post messages, and informing you how to unsubscribe. Keep that message!

Below are mailing lists that you might want to try out. I do not evaluate these lists. Some are active, others nearly dead. Some hold relatively conservative theological positions, while others are quite liberal — but almost always with exceptions. As always, *caveat emptor*. If you don't like the messages being posted on one of the lists, you can always unsubscribe. Most of the descriptions I give are summaries of the official descriptions given by the people who run the list. They may or may not reflect the real discussion that takes place on the list. The kind of discussion on a list is dynamic.

When you send your message to subscribe to a list, put in the body of the message only the information that I suggest in each listing (under "message to subscribe"). Be sure that you don't have anything else in your message, including any fancy "signatures," the graphics and address information that some people put at the end of their messages. Also, you must use the exact, abbreviated name of the list; I give these names in parenthesis following the longer, more descriptive name for each list.

If you have trouble subscribing to any list, send an inquiry to the "postmaster" (without quotation marks) at the list's computer address (i.e., substitute "postmaster" for the abbreviated name of the list address (e.g., "postmaster@gospelcom.net"). The postmaster is the person in charge of the computer that automates the list, and he or she will normally get back to you quickly. The following categories are not perfect, and I decided not to put individual lists in more than one category, so be sure to check out every category that might apply to you.

Remember: "subscription address" is where you send the e-mail message to subscribe. The "message to subscribe" is the message you put in your subscription e-mail (don't include anything else, not even a signature). The one-way lists send information to you, but you cannot distribute your messages directly to other subscribers. Enjoy!

Lists for All Christians

Internet for Christians Newsletter (IFC)

This is my own biweekly one-way list for news and comment on the latest developments in cyberspace.

subscription address: ifc-request@gospelcom.net

message to subscribe: SUBSCRIBE your e-mail address

(Note: you can also visit this site on the Web at **http://www.gospelcom.net/ifc**)

365 Days of Glory Email List (365 DAYS)

"Visions of Glory Online Magazine" list offers a daily meditation on the glorious nature of God and how He interacts with His people.

subscription address: MAJORDOMO@KLC.NB.NET

message to subscribe: SUBSCRIBE 365DAYS

AIDS Ministry Email List (Alert)

The Board for Human Care Ministries' list provides info and assistance with a distinctly Lutheran approach to those infected or affected by HIV/AIDS.

subscription address: MAILSERV@CRF.CUIS.EDU

message to subscribe: SUBSCRIBE ALERT

The All About Families Newsletter (FAMILY)

This weekly newsletter contains Christian marriage- and family-related articles written by Norman Bales and collected from various other sources.

subscription address: MCOC@MINDCHURCH.ORG

message to subscribe: SUBSCRIBE FAMILY

The Alpha Course Discussion List (ALPHA)

This list aids anyone who wants to understand the Christian faith.

subscription address: hub@xc.org

message to subscribe: SUBSCRIBE ALPHA

Apologia Report

This weekly research journal summarizes and reviews hundreds of magazines, journals, and news publications, identifying the most valuable resources to aid Christians as they encounter competing truth claims and seek to respond wisely.

Also, "Apologia Report" provides a free online discussion area for apologetics specialists. Sample issues of "Apologia Report" are available via email.

subscription address: HUB@XC.ORG

message to subscribe: INFO AR-SAMPLE
END

Ask the Pastor Email List

http://members.aol.com/walts9/askthepastor/home/

Walter Snyder, a Lutheran pastor, answers questions from readers in his weekly column. Topics are wide-ranging — some serious life and faith issues and some lighter themes. An answers archive is available on the Web. Send a general request to subscribe.

subscription address: XRYSOSTOM@AOL.COM

Bible (BIBLE)

For anyone interested in learning to study the Bible.

subscription address: majordomo@virginia.edu

message to subscribe: SUBSCRIBE BIBLE your e-mail address

Bible Study Email List (BIBLESTUDY - L)

http://www.isc-durant.com/lbaa/bible.htm

This list exchanges Bible-study lessons and discusses biblical topics.

subscription address: LISTSERV@LISTSERV.INDIANA.EDU

message to subscribe: SUB BIBLESTUDY-L YOURNAME

Bible-Trip Email List (BIBLE - TRIP)

The Bible Group's (Sonic@Fan.net) list discusses the Bible and periodically publishes a Bible prophesy series.

subscription address: SONIC@FAN.NET

message to subscribe: SUBSCRIBE BIBLE-TRIP

Brazilian Christians Email List (EVANGELICOS - L)

This list is for Gospel discussions in Portuguese.

subscription address: MAJORDOMO@SUMMER.COM.BR

message to subscribe: SUBSCRIBE EVANGELICOS-L

Brigada-Medical-Missions Email List

This list discusses medical missions and facilitates networking, mobilization and the distribution of resources.

subscription address: HUB@XC.ORG

message to subscribe: SUBSCRIBE BRIGADA-MEDICAL-MISSIONS

Call to Prayer (CTP)

CTP is a ministry of the International Bible Society (IBS) and provides a monthly prayer theme. Also, submit your prayer requests to (ibs@gospelcom.net), and the staff at IBS will pray with you.

subscription address: CTP-IBS-REQUEST@GOSPELCOM.NET

message to subscribe: SUBSCRIBE YOUREMAILADDRESS

Catholic Spirituality Discussion List (SPIRIT-L)

A forum on spirituality in secular life in the context of the Roman Catholic faith.

subscription address: listserv@american.edu

message to subscribe: SUBSCRIBE SPIRIT-L your name

Charlie Peacock List (PEACOCK-LIST)

Includes a moderated discussion of Charlie's music and the relationship between the Christian faith and art.

subscription address: listserv@netcentral.net

message to subscribe: SUBSCRIBE PEACOCK-LIST your full name

Christians Home Educating Young Adults Email List (C - HEYA)

Larry Wilson's (lwilson@xc.org) list discusses homeschooling junior and senior high school students.

subscription address: HUB@XC.ORG

message to subscribe: SUBSCRIBE C-HEYA

Christian Music List (CHRISTIAN-MUSIC-LIST)

A general discussion of contemporary Christian music.

subscription address: listserv@netcentral.net

message to subscribe: SUBSCRIBE CHRISTIAN-MUSIC-LIST your full name

Christian Music Email Digest (CHRISTIAN MUSIC EMAIL DIGEST)

This list discusses all styles of Christian music, combines messages daily, and sends them to you in digest format.

subscription address: MAJORDOMO@LISTSERV.PRODIGY.COM

message to subscribe: SUBSCRIBE CHRISTIANMUSIC-DIGEST

Chinese-American Christians Discussion List (CAC)

To discuss issues related to (but not limited to) Chinese-American Christians.

subscription address: LISTSERVER@BCCN.ORG

message to subscribe: SUBSCRIBE CAC YOURNAME

Christian Devotional Newsletter (VESSEL)

This list is published periodically and may include a verse of Scripture, a short devotional, or simply a timely word from the Lord.

subscription address: HUB@XC.ORG

message to subscribe: SUBSCRIBE VESSEL

Christian Educator Email List

Christian Educator is for Christians involved in secular and private school education.

subscription address: LISTSERV@ASSOCIATE.COM

message to subscribe: SUBSCRIBE CHRISTIANEDUCATOR

Christian Email Newsletter

"The Seeker" is a new bimonthly Christian email newsletter. It will feature several short articles that "try to look at life through a Christian viewpoint."

subscription address: WRITEWC@AOL.COM

message to subscribe: SUBSCRIBE--THE SEEKER

Christian Employment Email List

Christian Employment is for Christian employers and job-seekers.

subscription address: LISTSERV@ASSOCIATE.COM

message to subscribe: SUBSCRIBE CHRISTIANEMPLOYMENT YOURNAME

Christian Homeschooling List (HSTUAC)

For discussing the practical aspects of Christian homeschooling.

subscription address: listserv@vms1.cc.uop.edu

message to subscribe: SUBSCRIBE hstuac

Christian Music Discussion List (CHRISTIANMUSIC)

This list discusses all styles of Christian music.

subscription address: majordomo@listserv.prodigy.com

message to subscribe: SUBSCRIBE CHRISTIANMUSIC

Christian Recovery Discussion List (RECOVERY)

A discussion group for believers who are recovering from addiction and loss.

subscription address: hub@xc.org

message to subscribe: SUBSCRIBE RECOVERY your e-mail address

Christian Singles Discussion List

For discussion among Christian singles.

subscription address: LISTSERV@ASSOCIATE.COM

message to subscribe: SUBSCRIBE CHRISTIANSINGLES YOURNAME

Christian Singles List (CHRISTIAN_SINGLES)

For lively discussion of being single and singles' issues.

subscription address: majordomo@iclnet93.iclnet.org

message to subscribe: SUBSCRIBE CHRISTIAN_SINGLES

Christian Software News (CSN)

For news of Christian and Church-related software.

subscription address: hub@xc.org

message to subscribe: subscribe csn your e-mail address

Christian Testimony (Joy)

For sharing praise reports, testimonies and the like.

subscription address: hub@xc.org

message to subscribe: SUBSCRIBE joy your e-mail address

Christian Thought for the Day Email List (CTHOUGHT)

This list distributes a daily inspirational quote, accompanied by a prayer.

subscription address:
CTHOUGHT-REQUEST@SPERIENCE.COM

message to subscribe: SUBSCRIBE

Christian Unity (CHRISTIAN UNITY)

For open discussion of unity among denominations.

subscription address: listserv@associate.com

message to subscribe: SUBSCRIBE CHRISTIAN UNITY your name

Christian Women on the Net (Christian_Women)

For discussion among Christian women.

subscription address: majordomo@iclnet93.iclnet.org

message to subscribe: SUBSCRIBE Christian_Women

Christian Writers Group Email List (CWG)

Christian writers share ideas, tips, encouragement, and information.

subscription address: HUB@XC.ORG

message to subscribe: SUBSCRIBE CWG-LIST

ChristianNet Evangelical Christian News Email List (CN - WORLD)

This list delivers ChristianNet evangelical Christian news and info from around the world.

subscription address: LISTPROC@ASSOCIATE.COM

message to subscribe: SUBSCRIBE CN-WORLD YOURNAME

ChristianNet-Scotland Email List (CN-SCOTLAND)

This list delivers ChristianNet Scottish news and info for evangelical Christians.

subscription address: LISTPROC@ASSOCIATE.COM

message to subscribe: SUBSCRIBE CN-SCOTLAND YOURNAME

ChristianNet-UK Email List (CN - UK)

This list reports Christian news and information about activities in the United Kingdom.

subscription address: LISTPROC@ASSOCIATE.COM

message to subscribe: SUBSCRIBE CN-UK YOURNAME

Concordia Publishing House Forum (CPH)

For news and discussion of the products and services of Concordia Publishing House.

subscription address: mailserv@crf.cuis.edu

message to subscribe: SUBSCRIBE CPH

Conservative Christian Discussion List (CONCHR-L)

For discussion among theologically conservative Christians.

subscription address: listserv@vm.temple.edu

message to subscribe: SUBSCRIBE CONCHR-L your name

C.S. Lewis List (MERELEWIS)

For discussion of the life and works of C.S. Lewis.

subscription address: listserv@listserv.aol.com

message to subscribe: SUBSCRIBE merelewis YourFirstName YourLastName

Cults Email List (CULTS)

This list discusses cults, sects and heresies, especially those affecting the Christian church.

subscription address: LISTPROC@ETERNITYMAG.COM

message to subscribe:
SUBSCRIBE CULTS YOUREMAILADDRESS

Daily Devotionals for Men, Women, and Couples

These daily devotional for men, women, and couples, starts with the book of Genesis and reaches the book of Revelation by the year's end.

subscription address: RGRIBSTER@SOTA-OH.COM

message to subscribe: SUBSCRIBE MEN'S DEVOTIONAL or SUBSCRIBE WOMEN'S DEVOTIONAL or SUBSCRIBE COUPLE'S DEVOTIONAL or SUBSCRIBE ALL DEVOTIONALS

Daily Quiet Time Devotional (DQT)

Reprinted for IVP's Quiet Time Bibles.

subscription address: MAJORDOMO@GOSPELCOM.NET

message to subscribe: SUBSCRIBE dqt

Daily Wisdom Devotional Via E-mail (DW)

The Daily Wisdom devotional with evangelistic emphasis for new believers and seekers.

subscription address: MAJORDOMO@GOSPELCOM.NET

message to subscribe: SUBSCRIBE dw

Depression and Spirituality Discussion List (XN-DEPRESSION)

This list, originally formed to explore spiritual means of coping with depressive illnesses has been redefined to be ecumenical Christian.

subscription address: HUB@XC.ORG

message to subscribe: SUBSCRIBE XN-DEPRESSION

Discipleship Challenger Bible Study

Dan Jenkins' daily Bible study calls Christians to be missionaries where they live and work.

subscription address: EUTYCHUS@INFOBAHN.ICUBED.COM

message to subscribe: SUBSCRIBE THE DISCIPLESHIP CHALLENGER

Dream-Net Email List

This list invites Christians to share ministry ideas and dreams.

subscription address: HUB@XC.ORG

message to subscribe: SUBSCRIBE DREAM-NET END

ELCA Rural Ministry List (ELCASTAR)

This list discusses rural ministry and distributes the "Starlights" newsletter, along with announcements of national and regional rural ministry conferences and workshops.

**subscription address:
AUTOSHARE@RIP.PHYSICS.UNK.EDU**

message to subscribe: SUBSCRIBE ELCASTAR YOUR FIRSTNAME YOURLASTNAME

Email Tours of Christian Web Sites (BELIEVER)

"Believer's Weekly," published by The Village Chapel at WorldVillage, features an in-depth tour of one major Christian Web site each week.

**subscription address:
MAJORDOMO@WORLDVILLAGE.COM**

message to subscribe: SUBSCRIBE BELIEVER

Encouraging Words Email List (VOTD)

This list sends an inspirational message each weekday morning. Sources include contemporary and historical authors and lyricists, as well as quotes from the Bible.

subscription address: MAJORDOMO@BRUNERHAUS.COM

message to subscribe: SUBSCRIBE VOTD

Evangelism Discussion Forum (EVANGELISM)

For discussion of evangelism ideas, needs, concerns, experiences and resources.

subscription address: mailserv@crf.cuis.edu

message to subscribe: SUBSCRIBE EVANGELISM

"Experiencing God" Bible Study Via E-mail (EXPGOD)

Thomas Kennedy has set up an e-mail discussion list for the 13-week "Experiencing God" Bible study.

subscription address: hub@xc.org

message to subscribe: SUBSCRIBE EXPGOD

Friends of Amy Grant List (AMY-LIST)

A one-way list that enables the Friends of Amy Grant to send official messages to subscribers, including information about Amy's itineraries, announcements of new recordings, and media appearances.

subscription address: listserv@netcentral.net

message to subscribe: SUBSCRIBE AMY-LIST your full name

God-Talk Email List (GOD_TALK)

This list discusses Christianity.

subscription address: LISTPROC@ETERNITYMAG.COM

message to subscribe: SUBSCRIBE GOD_TALK YOUR EMAILADDRESS

Christian Graphics List (GODLYGRAPHICS)

Godly Graphics is for discussion and posts of non-copyrighted Christian art.

subscription address: LISTSERV@ASSOCIATE.COM

message to subscribe: SUBSCRIBE GODLYGRAPHICS YOURNAME

Gospel Communications Network Announcement List (GCN-ANNOUNCE)

A one-way list to notify Christians of new resources and information available on GCN's World Wide Web site, including new ministries that join the network.

subscription address: gcn-announce-request@gospelcom.net

message to subscribe: SUBSCRIBE your e-mail address

Gospel Music Email List (GOSPEL - L)

This list discusses gospel music.

subscription address: LISTSERV@LISTSERV.INDIANA.EDU

message to subscribe: SUB GOSPEL-L YOURNAME

GraceMail Email List

Receive lawyer and author Edward Fudge's daily, scripture-based articles by sending him a request at: EDWFUDGE@AOL.COM

Heartland Daily Devotion (TODAY'S VERSE)

Heartlight Magazine's daily devotional with scripture and prayer.

subscription address: todaysverse@heartlight.org

message to subscribe: SUBSCRIBE todaysverse

Hearts-Sanctuary (HEARTS-SANCTUARY)

A moderated list for prayer requests and for praise for prayers answered.

subscription address: listserv@listserv.aol.com

message to subscribe: SUBSCRIBE Hearts-Sanctuary yourfirst-name yourlastname

His-Net Newsletter

A monthly newsletter that features new Christian web sites.

subscription address: newsletter@his-net.com

message to subscribe: SUBSCRIBE

Home Church Discussion List (HCDL)

For home-church discussion.

subscription address: majordomo@shore.net

message to subscribe: subscribe hcdl

Illustrations Abound in E-Newsletter (THIS - IS - TRUE)

This is a weekly e-newsletter of strange but true news items —
a great resource for story illustrations.

subscription address: listserv@netcom.com

message to subscribe: SUBSCRIBE THIS-IS-TRUE

In Christ Ministries Devotional Via E-mail (DEVOTIONAL)

A daily e-mail devotional from ICM.

subscription address: kelly@inchrist.org

write DEVOTIONAL in subject line and YOUR-EMAIL-AD-
DRESS in body of e-mail.

International Christian Cycling Club (ICCC)

For uniting Christian cyclists worldwide in lifestyle, training and
sportsmanship.

subscription address: majordomo@cycling.org

message to subscribe: SUBSCRIBE ICCC

"Invisible-Concepts" Newsletter

This newsletter's articles help people apply biblical principles in the workplace.

subscription address: MAJORDOMO@IX.GEN.COM

message to subscribe: SUBSCRIBE INVISIBLE-CONCEPTS

"Invisible-Connections" Newsletter (INVISIBLE)

This newsletter provides timely and informative resources — articles, book reviews, devotional challenges, Bible studies — to help Christians in their walk and ministry.

subscription address: MAJORDOMO@IX.GEN.COM

message to subscribe: SUBSCRIBE INVISIBLE

Mission Support Network (JESUS - NET)

Evangelical missions information, including updates from the field and technology news.

subscription address: Jesus-Net@usa.net

John Stott Daily Devotional (STOTT)

Daily devotionals reprinted from Dr. Stott's books.

subscription address: MAJORDOMO@GOSPELCOM.NET

message to subscribe: SUBSCRIBE stott

Vegetarian Newsletter (JOHNNY APPLESEED)

The free monthly "Johnny Appleseed Newsletter" teaches vegetarian cooking from a Christian viewpoint. It also includes recipes and informational articles regarding vegetarian eating.

subscription address: BURNETTE@TELEVAR.COM

message to subscribe: SUBSCRIBE JOHNNY APPLESEED

Kids World Email List

A twelve-year-old, from Tasmania, Australia, set up this email list and sends weekly news and stories to other young Christians. To subscribe, send a request.

subscription address: RACHEL@TASSIE.NET.AU

King's College Discussion List (TKUCALUM)

This is an unofficial discussion group for alumni of The King's College/The King's University College (Edmonton).

subscription address: majordomo@debres.cuug.ab.ca

message to subscribe: SUBSCRIBE TKUCALUM

Kingdom Writers Email List (KINGWRIT)

This list provides critique and fellowship for Christian writers. All subscribers are required to submit a short biography before being added to the list.

subscription address: OWNER-KINGWRIT@NETSIDE.COM

message to subscribe: SUBSCRIBE KINGWRIT

Ladies Fellowship Email List

Ladies Fellowship is for women only to share and minister to one another.

subscription address: LISTSERV@ASSOCIATE.COM

message to subscribe: SUBSCRIBE LADIES_FELLOWSHIP YOURNAME

Lighthouse Electronic Magazine (LIGHTHOUSE-LIST)

Includes features, reviews and press releases pertaining to Contemporary Christian music.

subscription address: listserv@netcentral.net

message to subscribe: SUBSCRIBE LIGHTHOUSE-LIST your full name

Media Watch Email (MEDIAWATCH)

Media Watch reports news with a Godly perspective to counter-act media bias.

subscription address: LISTSERV@ASSOCIATE.COM

message to subscribe: SUBSCRIBE MEDIAWATCH YOURNAME

The Mind of Christ Email List (TMOC)

Based on Philippians 2:5-11, this email list teaches believers how to think the thoughts of Christ, or to have the mind of Christ.

subscription address: HUB@XC.ORG

message to subscribe: SUBSCRIBE TMOC

MissionNet

Dedicated to missions and the spread of the Gospel. To subscribe send a request.

subscription address: ron@missionnet.org

Music Ministry Email List (MUSIC-MINISTRY)

This list is a support forum for Christians who use music as their means of ministry — from choir directors to sound engineers, from recording artists to choir members.

subscription address: LISTSERV@ASSOCIATE.COM

message to subscribe: SUBSCRIBE MUSIC-MINISTRY YOURNAME

Newsletter for Christian Artists (CRA)

The Christian Reconstruction Art newsletter is for artists seeking to advance the Kingdom of God through their artwork. It inspires and provides resources and networking opportunities for Christian artists.

subscription address: BYNUMM@ICSI.NET

message to subscribe: INFO CRA

Ninos De Mexico Christian Children's Ministry (NINOS - L)

This list distributes news and prayer requests for the Ninos de Mexico Christian Children's Ministry near Mexico City.

subscription address: MAJORDOMO@JBU.EDU

message to subscribe: SUBSCRIBE NINOS-L

Practical Christian Life List (CHRISTIA)

For discussion of living the Christian life.

subscription address: listserv@asuvm.inre.asu.edu

message to subscribe: SUBSCRIBE CHRISTIA your name

The Prayer Conference (PRAYER)

This list unites Christians from around the world "to be a house for prayer for people from all nations" (Mark 11:17).

subscription address: HUB@XC.ORG

message to subscribe: SUBSCRIBE PRAYER

Prayer & Memorial Requests (CCP - TACOMA)

Prayer requests and updates.

subscription address: LISTSERV@LISTSERV.AOL.COM

message to subscribe: SUBSCRIBE CCP-TACOMA "YOUR FIRST NAME" "YOUR LAST NAME"

Prayer Partners

A moderated list to help Christian school ministries (K-12) through networking.

subscription address: HUB@XC.ORG

message to subscribe: SUBSCRIBE PRAYER-PARTNERS

Promise Keepers

For fellowship and encouragement of dedicated Christian men. (Not affiliated with Promise Keepers.)

subscription address: HUB@XC.ORG

message to subscribe: SUBSCRIBE PK

Promise Keeping Men Discussion List

Promise Keeping Men is for fellowship and encouragement of dedicated Christian men. (Not affiliated with Promise Keepers.)

subscription address: LISTSERV@ASSOCIATE.COM

message to subscribe: SUBSCRIBE PROMISE-KEEPING_MEN YOURNAME

Promise Keepers Official Ministry Update List

Receive important PK ministry updates.

**subscription address:
PKINFO-REQUEST@PROMISEKEEPERS.ORG**

message to subscribe: SUBSCRIBE

Promise Keepers Official Prayer List

Receive PK prayer requests and praise items.

**subscription address:
PKPRAYER-REQUEST@PROMISEKEEPERS.ORG**

message to subscribe: SUBSCRIBE

Religious Fiction Email List (HOLYFIC)

This list is for posting Christian fantasy fiction or fiction with religion as a major theme.

subscription address: LISTSERV@VM.TEMPLE.EDU

message to subscribe: SUB HOLYFIC YOURFIRSTNAME YOURLASTNAME

SchoolWatch Newsletter

Each weekly SchoolWatch newsletter highlights new and interesting educational Web sites, including family-friendly sites for kids to explore.

subscription address: MATRIX@PE.NET

message to subscribe: SUBSCRIBE SCHOOLWATCH

Signs of the Times Email List

This list deals with prophecy of the end times.

subscription address: SIGNS@CWINET.ORG

message to subscribe: SUBSCRIBE

Spurgeon Devotional List (MORNING-EVENING-DEVOTIONAL)

For receiving the morning and evening devotional of C.H. Spurgeon.

subscription address: majordomo@netpath.net

message to subscribe: subscribe morning-evening-devotional

Stott Bible Study (SBS)

An in-depth study of scripture using Dr. Stott's commentaries.

subscription address: MAJORDOMO@GOSPELCOM.NET

message to subscribe: SUBSCRIBE sbs

Study Hosea Via Email

The course, developed by Rev. Mark Perkins, pastor of Denver Bible Church, provides a grammatical and syntactical study to support an explanation and application of the principles of the book of Hosea. To subscribe, send a request to the following address.

subscription address: wdoud@bga.com

Taize Community "Johannine Hours" Email List (TAIZE - L)

Receive a short, monthly, biblical meditation prepared by one of the brothers of the ecumenical community of Taize in France.

subscription address: LISTSERV@RZ.UNI-KARLSRUHE.DE

message to subscribe: SUBSCRIBE TAIZE-L YOURFIRSTNAME YOURLASTNAME

Technology in the Church (TICTALK)

Technology in Christianity International Help Desk (TICTALK) Techno-missionaries answer questions on roles and practical applications of technologies for church, parachurch and missions.

subscription address: info@tictalk,org

message to subscribe: <leave subject and body blank>

Today's Thought by John Stott (TT)

A brief morning devotional to help focus your day on God.

subscription address: MAJORDOMO@GOSPELCOM.NET

message to subscribe: SUBSCRIBE tt

Toybox Charity Email List

This list distributes news and prayer requests for *Toybox Charity*, a ministry to the street children of Latin America.

subscription address: MAJORDOMO@JBU.EDU

message to subscribe: SUBSCRIBE TOYBOX-L

Train_Up Discussion List (TRAIN_UP)

A moderated list to help Christian school ministries (K-12) through networking.

subscription address: majordomo@iclnet93.iclnet.org

message to subscribe: SUBSCRIBE TRAIN_UP your e-mail address

The Way of Grace Fellowship Email List

This list, provides daily, morning and evening devotional messages and a place to share prayer needs and praise reports.

**subscription address:
Way-Of-Grace-Fellowship-request@UserHome.Com**

message to subscribe: SUBSCRIBE

WebWatch Newsletter

A weekly newsletter, published by the *Maranatha Christian Journal*, provides current news headlines and unearths Christian Internet sites which are unusual, creative, and thought-provoking. All entries reviewed by a volunteer board.

subscription address: MATRIX@PE.NET

message to subscribe: SUBSCRIBE WEBWATCH

Wit & Wisdom

A weekday mailing of wisdom, humor, trivia and spiritual thoughts.

subscription address: hub@xc.org

message to subscribe: SUBSCRIBE WIT-WISDOM

Word for Today Daily Email Devotional (WFT)

The devotional is published in printed form by United Christian Broadcasters of Europe.

subscription address: LISTPROC@ASSOCIATE.COM

message to subscribe: SUBSCRIBE WFT YOURNAME

World Vision Global Supporter Network (W-VISION)

This list is a meeting place and resource for World Vision supporters and friends of World Vision, an international, Christian, humanitarian organization.

subscription address: LISTPROC@SOLAR.RTD.UTK.EDU

message to subscribe: SUBSCRIBE W-VISION YOURNAME

Zondervan Publishing House's E-Mail Alert Service (EMAS)

Receive customized info about the numerous resources available from Zondervan Publishing House.

subscription address: lists@info.harpercollins.com

message to subscribe: SUBSCRIBE ZPHLIST

Lists for Ministry Leaders, including Parish Pastors, Student Leaders, Chaplains and Missionaries

Prison Outreach List (ACTS - CHAPLAINS)

The American Chaplaincy Training School, located at Taylor University in Fort Wayne, Indiana, has created an email list for those interested in ministering to the incarcerated, to families of the incarcerated, or to communities attempting to work with at-risk populations.

subscription address: MAJORDOMO@GOSPELCOM.NET

message to subscribe: SUBSCRIBE ACTS-CHAPLAINS-LIST

Call to Prayer (CTP - IBS)

CTP is a ministry of the International Bible Society (IBS), and provides a monthly prayer theme. Also, submit your prayer requests to ibs@gospelcom.net and the staff at IBS will pray with you.

subscription address:
CTP-IBS-REQUEST@GOSPELCOM.NET

message to subscribe: SUBSCRIBE YOUREMAILADDRESS

Catholic Campus Ministry List (NEWMAN-L)

For discussion of Catholic campus ministry.

subscription address: listserv@american.edu

message to subscribe: SUBSCRIBE NEWMAN-L your name

Computer-Aided Ministry (CAMSOC-UPDATE)

For information about computing and telecommunications, especially topics of interest to Christians.

subscription address: hub@xc.org

message to subscribe: SUBSCRIBE CAMSOC-UPDATE your e-mail address

Contents (CONTENTS)

Information for parish clergy and other ministries, including sermon notes/ideas; discussions of pastoral/leadership/ethical/ worship issues; theological articles.)

subscription address: clergym@pastornet.net.au

message to subscribe: SUBSCRIBE (in the subject line)

Christians Teaching English as a Second Language (CTESL-L)

For Christians teaching English as a Second Language.

subscription address: Mail-Server@rhesys.mb.ca

message to subscribe: subscribe ctesl-l

Cell Church Discussion Group List (CELL-CHURCH)

A moderated list for discussion of cell churches, in which small numbers of believers meet in homes and other special locations.

subscription address: cell-church-request@bible.acu.edu

message to subscribe: SUBSCRIBE your name

Coalition of Christian Colleges & Universities The News

News about the over 90 Christian colleges in the CCCU.

subscription address: MAJORDOMO @GOSPELCOM.NET

message to subscribe: SUBSCRIBE CCCU-THE-NEWS

Christian Educator Discussion List

This list is for Christians involved in secular and private school education.

subscription address: LISTSERV@ASSOCIATE.COM

message to subscribe: SUBSCRIBE CHRISTIANEDUCATOR YOURNAME

Christian Missions Mail List (MISSIONNET)

A moderated list to facilitate and support Christian missions activity worldwide.

subscription address: majordomo@iclnet93.iclnet.org

message to subscribe: SUBSCRIBE MISSIONNET your e-mail address

Church Music (CHURCHMUSIC -L)

Planning music for the rites is challenging at the best of times. Subscribers to churchmusic-l will be able to give and get help on appropriate hymns, anthems and liturgical music.

Subscription address: majordomo@churchoffice.com

Message to subscribe:
subscribe churchmusic-l your@e-mail.address

ChurchOffice

This list will give practical advice on implementing new technology in service of the church, and reflect on theological and pastoral issues raised by implementing this new technology.

Subscription address: majordomo@churchoffice.com

Message to subscribe:
subscribe churchoffice your@e-mail.address

Churchplanters in Christianity List (CHURCHPLANTERS)

To encourage and assist people who share the goal of Christian churchplanting.

**subscription address:
churchplanters-request@genesis.acu.edu**

message to subscribe: SUBSCRIBE

Cross-Cultural Missions Email List (CMDNET)

The Centre for Mission Direction's information and news of missions resources among those in New Zealand, Australia, Asia and beyond.

subscription address: HUB@XC.ORG

message to subscribe: SUBSCRIBE BRIGADA-ORGS-CMDNET

Directory of Christian Organizations in Singapore (DCOS)

Maintained by Hylanders Mission Priority, this list offers free listings to global ministries, missions agencies, etc. For details and a blank listings form, send a message-less email to the following subscription address:

subscription address: DCOS@LIONCITY.COM

Deaf Ministries Discussion List

Deaf Ministries is for discussion of ministries conducted by the deaf community.

subscription address: LISTSERV@ASSOCIATE.COM

message to subscribe:
SUBSCRIBE DEAFMINISTRIES YOURNAME

Evangelism (EVANGELISM - L)

Subscribers to this list can find answers to questions like, what is needed to run an effective congregational evangelism program? Where does one turn for resources? How does one remain true to one's theological tradition building an evangelism program? How can a sense of being evangelists be instilled in the life of the church?

Subscription address: majordomo@churchoffice.com

Message to subscribe:
subscribe evangelism-l your@e-mail.address

GADARENE LIST (GADARENE-L)

For prayer, support, comfort and acceptance for those with chronic mental illness, and for their family and friends.

subscription address: hub@xc.org

message to subscribe: subscribe Gadarene-L

Christian Ideas List (Idea - Central)

Idea-Central serves as a clearinghouse of Christian ideas for pastors, writers, speakers, Bible study teachers, and others.

subscription address: ListServ@associate.com

message to subscribe: Subscribe Idea-Central YOURNAME

InterVarsity Christian Fellowship Discussion List (IVCF-L)

For discussion related to this multi-denominational Christian campus group.

subscription address: listserv@ubvm.cc.buffalo.edu

message to subscribe: SUBSCRIBE IVCF-L your name

Leadership (LEADERSHIP- L)

Board chairpersons and members ask: how do we effectively lead the church, support the staff, make the organization work, and still witness to Christ.

Subscription address: majordomo@churchoffice.com

Message to subscribe:
subscribe leadership-l your@e-mail.address

Leadership Forum List (LEADERSHIP)

To help Christian leaders in ministry network around the globe.

subscription address: majordomo@iclnet93.iclnet.org

message to subscribe: SUBSCRIBE LEADERSHIP your e-mail address

Ministers and Ministry Discussion List (MINISTRY)

For discussion of the daily concerns of ministers, including non-parish ministry.

subscription address: listserv@ls.csbsju.edu

message to subscribe: SUBSCRIBE MINISTRY your name

Mission and Church-Planting News with the Dawn Friday Fax

The Dawn Friday Fax contains weekly updates on mission and church-planting successes around the world.

subscription address: FF-LISTSERV@MACIMS1.NTB.CH

message to subscribe: SUBSCRIBE FRIDAYFAX YOURFIRST-NAME YOURLASTNAME

Monday Morning Reality Check (REALITY-CHECK)

A weekly report on worldwide missions as reported by David B. Barrett and the Global Evangelization Movement.

subscription address: hub@xc.org

message to subscribe: subscribe reality-check your e-mail address

Music-Ministry Email List

This list is for discussion among Christians who minister through music.

subscription address: LISTPROC@ASSOCIATE.COM

message to subscribe: SUBSCRIBE MUSIC-MINISTRY YOUR-NAME

Network of Single Adult Leaders Email List (NSL -DL)

This list is for discussion among single-adult ministry leaders.

subscription address: MAJORDOMO@GOSPELCOM.NET

message to subscribe: SUBSCRIBE NSL-DL

North American Missions Prayer List (STN-NA)

This is a missionary prayer list for North America, sponsored by LutherNet.

subscription address: mailserv@crf.cuis.edu

message to subscribe: SUBSCRIBE STN-NA

Preaching the Revised Common Lectionary List (PRCL-L)

For clergy from different traditions to study and discuss the Lectionary and its use.

subscription address: listserv@ulkyvm.louisville.edu

message to subscribe: SUBSCRIBE PRCL-L your name

Sermon Outlines (SERMONSEEDS)

A weekly mailing of brief expository sermon outlines by Pastor Jack Peters. To subscribe send a request.

subscription address: jpeters@klink.net

Support for Pastors (PASTORS)

For pastors to pray for one another, share their joys and frustrations, share sermon notes, and the like.

subscription address: hub@xc.org

message to subscribe: subscribe pastors

Office Secretary (SECRETARY - L)

Running an office efficiently, making purchase decisions and handling those omnipresent church politics is enough for any church secretary to join this list.

subscription address: majordomo@churchoffice.com

message to subscribe: subscribe secretary-l your@e-mail.address

Social Ministry (SOCIALMINISTRY - L)

Subscribers can network globally to help each other interpret and implement the "gospel imperative" in the congregations. The network can also address critical issues and mobilize resources quickly as need arises.

Subscription address: majordomo@churchoffice.com

message to subscribe:
subscribe socialministry-l your@e-mail.address

Stewardship (STEWARDSHIP - L)

How does one develop and run a church stewardship program? Where does one turn for resources? How does one remain true to one's theological tradition while building a stewardship pro-gram? How can the sense of Christian stewardship be instilled in the life of the church? These issues and more find resolution for subscribers of stewardship-l.

Subscription address: majordomo@churchoffice.com

message to subscribe:
subscribe stewardship-l your@e-mail.address

Sunday School (SUNDAYSCHOOL - L)

Teachers and directors of learning ministries can get helpful ideas on designing successful lesson plans, getting ideas on particular issues and topics and collaborate on raising the importance of the life-long learning ministry in the church.

Subscription address: majordomo@churchoffice.com

message to subscribe:
subscribe sundayschool-l your@e-mail.address

Missions List for Africa, the Middle East and Asia Minor (Ten40-L)

This list, arranged and sponsored by Hylanders Mission Priority, supports ministries in "World A" (those who have not heard the Gospel) regions just west of Asia, within the 10/40 Window of opportunity. Participation is restricted to missionaries and serious intercessors. To subscribe, send a request to the following address.

subscription address: CHAT.TEN40-L@LIONCITY.COM

Theology Email List

This list is for thoughtful discussion dealing with the characteristics of God.

subscription address: LISTSERV@ASSOCIATE.COM

message to subscribe: SUBSCRIBE THEOLOGY YOURNAME

The Timothy Report Email List

This list (SmH255@aol.com) delivers weekly sermon illustrations and ideas.

subscription address: SWANLC@AOL.COM

message to subscribe: SUBSCRIBE NEW TIMOTHY TRIAL

Finance Officers (TREASURER-1)

Subscribers will learn from lay and professional accountants how to adapt to changes wrought by national church offices or governments.

Subscription address: majordomo@churchoffice.com

message to subscribe: subscribe treasurer-l your@e-mail.address

Urban Ministry Forum (CITYFISH)

An ecumenical forum for exchanging ideas and issues about urban ministry.

subscription address: mailserv@crf.cuis.edu

message to subscribe: SUBSCRIBE CITYFISH

Women-In-Ministry Discussion List (WOMEN-IN-MINISTRY)

This list addresses the unique needs of Christian women called to or active in ministry, providing support, mentoring, and encouragement.

subscription address: MAJORDOMO@NEWLIFEBEGINS.COM

message to subscribe: INFO WOMEN-IN-MINISTRY

Worship Resources (WORSHIP-FAQ)

A monthly update on worship resources.

subscription address: listproc@grmi.org

message to subscribe: subscribe worship-faq Firstname Lastname

Worship Topics (WORSHIP)

For discussing multi-denominational worship topics.

subscription address: listproc@grmi.org

message to subscribe: subscribe worship FirstName LastName

Youth (YOUTH - 1)

Youth ministry people can consult on their work, get an appreciation for youth ministry in a global setting and arrange international youth exchanges to develop a better understanding of the whole Body of Christ.

Subscription address: majordomo@churchoffice.com

message to subscribe: subscribe youth-l your@e-mail.address

Youth Ministries Forum (YOUTHMINISTRY-L)

An online community of youth workers who want to guide, encourage and assist each other in their ministry to teenagers.

subscription address: youthministry-l-request@gospelcom.net

message to subscribe: SUBSCRIBE your e-mail address

Youth With a Mission International News Digest (YWAM-NEWS)

For news about missions outreach.

subscription address: hub@xc.org

message to subscribe: subscribe ywam-news your e-mail address

Lists for Christian Scholars and Other Academic-Minded Folks, including Theologians

Acts Study List (ACTS-L)

For the scholarly study of the Gospel of Luke and the Acts of the Apostles.

subscription address: listserv@listserv.uottawa.ca

message to subscribe: subscribe ACTS-L your name

American Religious History Discussion List (H-AMREL)

To foster discussion on issues of methodology, historiography and teaching ideas/methods relating to all aspects of American religious history.

subscription address: listserv@msu.edu

message to subscribe: SUBSCRIBE H-AMREL your name

Apologia Report

This new, weekly, online research journal summarizes and reviews hundreds of magazines, journals, and news publications, identifying the most valuable resources to aid Christians as they encounter competing truth claims and seek to respond wisely.

subscription address: HUB@XC.ORG

message to subscribe: INFO AR-SAMPLE END

Biblical Hebrew Studies List (B-HEBREW)

Sponsored by the Center for Christian Study, to foster communication concerning the scholarly study of the Hebrew Bible.

subscription address: majordomo@virginia.edu

message to subscribe: SUBSCRIBE B-HEBREW

Medical-Missions Email List

Discusses medical missions and facilitates networking, mobilization and the distribution of resources.

subscription address: HUB@XC.ORG

message to subscribe:
SUBSCRIBE BRIGADA-MEDICAL-MISSIONS

Christians Home Educating Young Adults Email List

Larry Wilson's (lwilson@xc.org) list discusses homeschooling junior and senior high school students.

subscription address: HUB@XC.ORG

message to subscribe: SUBSCRIBE C-HEYA

Christian Learning List (FAITH-LEARNING)

To encourage creative thinking and leadership among Christian educators seeking to integrate religious faith with teaching, learning and scholarship.

subscription address: mailserv@baylor.edu

message to subscribe: SUBSCRIBE FAITH-LEARNING yourname

Christianity and Literature Discussion List (CHRISTLIT)

To discuss the interrelations between Christianity and literature.

subscription address: listserv@bethel.edu

message to subscribe: SUBSCRIBE CHRISTLIT your name

Dietrich Bonhoeffer/Paul Tillich E-mail List (DBPT-L)

This list discusses "Theology and Cultural Criticism," focusing on the work of Dietrich Bonhoeffer and Paul Tillich.

subscription address: listproc2@bgu.edu

message to subscribe: SUBSCRIBE DBPT-L your name

A Digital Theology Newsletter (ECCAST - L)

This newsletter is for anyone interested in Digital and Model Theology.

subscription address: listproc2@bgu.edu

message to subscribe: SUBSCRIBE ECCHST-L your name

Eternity Online Magazine Exegesis Email List

This list discusses obscure or difficult biblical texts.

subscription address: LISTPROC@ETERNITYMAG.COM

message to subscribe: SUBSCRIBE EXEGESIS

Evangelicals In Religious Studies Email List

This list is for discussion among evangelical Christians in the field of religious studies.

subscription address: RUSSR@INAV.NET

message to subscribe: SUBSCRIBE

Include the following info in the body of the email: name, email address, school and degree program, research interests, denominational or theological affiliation

George MacDonald Email List

This list is devoted to the life and work of George MacDonald (1824-1905), author of major works of fantasy such as "Phantastes," "Lilith," the Curdie books and "The Golden Key," and a major influence on C.S. Lewis.

subscription address: PARTRIDGE@DIAL.PIPEX.COM

message to subscribe: MACDONALD

Gospel of John Discussion List (JOHNLITR)

A forum for dialogue about the Fourth Gospel.

subscription address: listserv@univscvm.csd.scarolina.edu

message to subscribe: SUBSCRIBE JOHNLITR your name

Greek New Testament List (B-GREEK)

To foster communication about the scholarly study of the Greek New Testament.

subscription address: majordomo@virginia.edu

message to subscribe: SUBSCRIBE B-GREEK your e-mail address

Greek Questions Email List

This list discusses the interpretation and application of the Greek biblical text.

subscription address:
GREEK-QUESTIONS-REQUEST@GENESIS.ACU.EDU

message to subscribe: SUBSCRIBE

Hebrew Old Testament (B-HEBREW)

For the scholarly study of the Hebrew Old Testament.

subscription address: majordomo@virginia.edu

message to subscribe: SUBSCRIBE B-HEBREW your e-mail address

History of American Catholicism (AMERCATH)

To discuss all aspects of the history of Catholicism in America.

subscription address: listserv@ukcc.uky.edu

message to subscribe: SUBSCRIBE AMERCATH your name

Holy Spirit Outpourings Email List

For discussion of the Holy Spirit.

To subscribe, send a request to: SHARLOW@WAVE.NET

Idea-Central Email List

Idea-Central serves as a clearinghouse of ideas for pastors, Christian writers, Christian speakers, Bible study teachers, etc.

subscription address: ListServ@associate.com

message to subscribe: Subscribe Idea-Central

Liturgy Discussion List (LITURGY)

To discuss all aspects of the academic study of Christian liturgy.

subscription address: mailbase@mailbase.ac.uk

message to subscribe: SUBSCRIBE LITURGY your name

Pew Scholars Email List (NPEW - L)

This list is for information about Pew scholarships, fellowships, and other info of interest to Christian academics.

subscription address: LISTSERV@VMA.CC.ND.EDU

message to subscribe: SUBSCRIBE NDPEW-L YOURNAME

Reformed Theology (REFORMED)

For discussion of all things Calvinist.

subscription address: listserv@listserv.syr.edu

message to subscribe: subscribe Reformed your name

Science and Christianity List (SCICHR-L)

A moderated forum for the discussion of the relationship between science and Christianity.

subscription address: send note requesting subscription to the moderator (schimmri@hercules.geology.uiuc.edu)

"Sightings" Email Newsletter — Martin Marty

From the Public Religion Project, directed by venerable University of Chicago professor Martin Marty, this newsletter features current events involving the relation between religion and the public sphere. To subscribe, send a request (including your name and organization) to:

PRP-INFO@PUBLICRELIGIONPROJ.ORG

Society of Christian Philosophers Email List (SCP)

http://www.siu.edu/departments/cola/philos/SCP/

The Society of Christian Philosophers promotes fellowship among Christian philosophers and stimulates study and discussion of the nature and role of Christian commitment in philosophy. This list sends SCP news, announcements of conferences, calls for papers, requests for information, and items for philosophical discussion.

subscription address: SCP-OWNER@CALVIN.EDU

message to subscribe: SUBSCRIBE SCP

Sola Doctrines Email List (SOLA)

For discussion of the "SOLA" doctrines of the Reformation: Sola Scriptura, Solus Christus, Sola Fide, Sola Gratia, and Sola Deo Gloria.

subscription address: MAJORDOMO@TAO.AGORON.COM

message to subscribe: SUBSCRIBE SOLA YOUR EMAIL ADDRESS

Theology Discussion List (THEOLOGY)

This list is for thoughtful discussion of the characteristics of God.

subscription address: LISTSERV@ASSOCIATE.COM

message to subscribe: SUBSCRIBE THEOLOGY YOURNAME

Theology Discussion List (THEOLOGY)

To foster friendly discussion and debate within evangelical theology.

subscription address: majordomo@iclnet.org

message to subscribe: SUBSCRIBE THEOLOGY YOURE-MAILADDRESS

Wittenberg List (WITTENBERG)

For discussion of Lutheran Church History.

subscription address: mailserv@crf.cuis.edu

message to subscribe: SUBSCRIBE WITTENBERG YOURNAME

Lists for Christian Traditions

Anabaptist Discussion (ANABAPTIST - TALK)

A small, friendly list for discussing issues important to those or of interested in the Anabaptist faith.

subscription address: HUB@XC.ORG

message to subscribe: SUBSCRIBE ANABAPTIST-TALK

Anglican List (ANGLICAN)

For open discussions relating to the Episcopalian Church.

subscription address: listserv@american.edu

message to subscribe: SUBSCRIBE ANGLICAN your name

Associate Reformed Presbyterian List (ARP-CHURCH)

This is a moderated Internet e-mail discussion list devoted to news and issues about the Associate Reformed Presbyterian Church around the world.

subscription address: kmcmulle@mail.win.org

message to subscribe: SUBSCRIBE ARP-CHURCH your name

Baptist List (BAPTIST)

For open discussion of all topics relating to Baptist experience.

subscription address: listserv@lsv.uky.edu

message to subscribe: SUBSCRIBE BAPTIST your name

Canadian Lutheran List (ELC-CANADA)

For members and others interested in the theology, practice and issues of the Evangelical Lutheran Church in Canada.

subscription address: listproc@gpfn.sk.ca

message to subscribe: subscribe elc-canada your name

Canadian Anglican Forum (CANANG-L)

For discussion of Canadian Anglican issues.

subscription address: listserv@pdomain.uwindsor.ca

message to subscribe: subscribe canang-l your name

Canadian Baptist Discussion (CBAP-L)

For friendly discussion among Canadian Baptists.

subscription address: maiser@kingsu.ab.ca

message to subscribe: SUBSCRIBE CBAP-L

Catholic Discussion (CATH-L)

For open Catholic discussion.

subscription address: listserv@american.edu

message to subscribe: SUBSCRIBE CATH-L your name

Catholic Reform and Renewal List (RENEW-L)

For discussion of reform and renewal in Catholicism.

subscription address: listserv@american.edu

message to subscribe: SUBSCRIBE RENEW-L your name

Christian Church Discussion List

For members and friends of the Christian Church.

subscription address: LISTSERV@ASSOCIATE.COM

message to subscribe: SUBSCRIBE CC YOURNAME

Christian Reconstruction Email List (CH - RECON)

http://www.geocities.com/Athens/6207

For discussion among Christian Reconstructionists, who hold five main distinctives: Calvinism, presuppositional apologetics, theonomy, postmillennialism, and dominionism.

subscription address:
MAJORDOMO@MAJORDOMO.POBOX.COM

message to subscribe: SUBSCRIBE CH-RECON

Christian Reformed Church Webmaster Email List

The webmaster of the Christian Reformed Church, established this mailing list to assist churches in building and maintaining web sites.

subscription address: MAJORDOMO@CALVIN.EDU

message to subscribe: SUBSCRIBE CRC-WEBMASTER

Church of Christ Youth Ministry List (YOUTHMIN-L)

To connect youth ministers around the country.

subscription address: youthmin-l-request@nicanor.acu.edu

message to subscribe: subscribe

Church of God Discussion List (COG)

For Church of God members and friends.

subscription address: LISTSERV@ASSOCIATE.COM

message to subscribe: SUBSCRIBE COG YOURNAME

Episcopal Discussion List (EPISCOPAL)

For discussion of the Episcopal church and the Episcopal Diocese of Washington (DC).

subscription address: majordomo@list.us.net

message to subscribe: SUBSCRIBE EPISCOPAL

The Estonian Lutheran Church Email List (EELK - L)

This list discusses (primarily in English) ecumenical issues, youth ministry, and more.

subscription address:
MAJORDOMO@CHURCHOFFICE.COM

message to subscribe: SUBSCRIBE EELK-L

Evangelical Lutheran Church in America Discussion List (ELCA-L)

A forum for the discussion of issues relevant to the Evangelical Lutheran Church in America.

subscription address: listproc2@bgu.edu

message to subscribe: SUBSCRIBE ELCA-L your name

Free Catholic List (CATHOLIC)

For Catholic discussion.

subscription address: listserv@american.edu

message to subscribe: SUBSCRIBE CATHOLIC your name

Independent Baptist Missions Conference (IBMISSIONS)

A moderated conference for Independent Baptists to inform each other of missionary needs and accomplishments.

subscription address: hub@xc.org

message to subscribe:
SUBSCRIBE IBMISSIONS your e-mail address

Independent Catholic and Orthodox List (IND-CATH)

For discussion of Independent Catholic and Orthodox matters.

subscription address: majordomo@wave.rio.com

message to subscribe: subscribe ind-cath your e-mail address

Lay-Clerks Email List

http://www.ncl.ac.uk/~n211552/lay-clerks.html

For discussion among lay clerks (and choral scholars, lay vicars, vicars choral, etc.) in UK cathedral and collegiate choirs.

subscription address: MAILBASE@NCL.AC.UK

message to subscribe: JOIN LAY-CLERKS YOURNAME

Lutheran List (LTHRN-L)

For discussion of issues relevant to the Lutheran Church.

subscription address: majordomo@tdkcs.waterloo.on.ca

message to subscribe: SUBSCRIBE LTHRN-L

Lutheran Family Email List (LUTHFAM)

The Lutheran Family Association's list discusses ideas to enhance ministry to families.

subscription address: MAILSERV@CRF.CUIS.EDU

message to subscribe: SUBSCRIBE LUTHFAM

LutherNet's Email Lists

LutherNet offers email lists covering topics like evangelism, missions, sermons, the HIV/AIDS pandemic, black ministry, Church history, urban ministry, Christian publications, disaster response, church news and schedules, daily devotions, family life, youth ministry, and more.

subscription address: MAILSERV@CRF.CUIS.EDU

message for detailed info about all of the lists, including how to subscribe:
LISTS
HELP

Mennonite Lists

Get a list of the many email lists covering topics related to the Anabaptist/Mennonite faith.

subscription address: server@mennolink.org

message to subscribe: INFO

Nazarene Church Email List (NAZARENE)

This list is for members and friends of the Nazarene church.

subscription address: LISTSERV@ASSOCIATE.COM

message to subscribe: SUBSCRIBE NAZARENE YOURNAME

Stone-Campbell List (STONE-CAMPBELL)

For discussion of the Restoration Movement, including the Churches of Christ, the independent Christian Churches and the Disciples of Christ.

subscription address: stone-campbell-request@bible.acu.edu

message to subscribe: SUBSCRIBE STONE-CAMPBELL your name

Orthodox (ORTHODOX)

For discussion relating to Orthodox Christianity and the Eastern Orthodox Church.

subscription address: listserv@iubvm.ucs.indiana.edu

message to subscribe: SUBSCRIBE ORTHODOX YourFirstName YourLastName

Catholic Parish Email List (PARISH - L)

This list is for deacons, members of religious orders and congregations, and lay persons who are parish administrators/directors/managers in Roman Catholic parishes in the U.S. and Canada.

subscription address: LISTSERV@LS.CSBSJU.EDU

message to subscribe: SUBSCRIBE PARISH-L YOURFIRSTNAME YOURFAMILYNAME

Reformation Email List (REFORMATION)

http://www.iserv.net/~dknight/ref/faq.html

This list discusses the Reformed Church in America.

subscription address: LISTSERV@BAKERBOOKS.COM

message to subscribe: SUBSCRIBE REFORMATION YOURFIRSTNAME YOURLASTNAME

United Methodist Disciple Bible Study (UMD)

UMD is an unmoderated discussion of the United Methodist Disciple Bible Study courses, which are offered worldwide.

**subscription address:
LISTSERV@MAELSTROM.STJOHNS.EDU**

message to subscribe: SUBSCRIBE UMD YOURFIRSTNAME YOURLASTNAME

United Methodist List (UM-LIST)

For discussion of United Methodism.

subscription address: listserv@ulkyvm.louisville.edu

message to subscribe: subscribe UM-LIST

Where Can I Find More Mailing Lists?

Subscribe to my free newsletter (see the "Lists for all Christians" section of the appendix) or visit the Internet for Christians site (http://www.gospelcom.net/ifc) for updates on Christian-oriented lists. If you'd like to search for additional lists on other, non-Christian topics, use these sites:

Liszt Mailing List Directory

http://www.liszt.com/

Reference.com

http://www.reference.com

E-Mail discussion Groups

http://albanza.com/kabacoff/Inter-Links/listserv.html

GOSPEL FILMS

PUBLICATIONS